NEW
SUPERVISOR
training

MW01256488

ATD Workshop Series

NEW SUPERVISOR
training

ELAINE BIECH

atd
PRESS
Alexandria, Virginia

© 2015 ASTD DBA Association for Talent Development (ATD)
All rights reserved. Printed in the United States of America.

18 17 16 15   1 2 3 4 5

No part of this publication may be reproduced, distributed, or transmitted in any form or by any means, including photocopying, recording, or other electronic or mechanical methods, without the prior written permission of the publisher, except in the case of brief quotations embodied in critical reviews and certain other noncommercial uses permitted by copyright law. For permission requests, please go to www.copyright.com, or contact Copyright Clearance Center (CCC), 222 Rosewood Drive, Danvers, MA 01923 (telephone: 978.750.8400; fax: 978.646.8600).

ATD Press is an internationally renowned source of insightful and practical information on talent development, workplace learning, and professional development.

ATD Press
1640 King Street Box 1443
Alexandria, VA 22313-1443 USA

Ordering information for print edition: Books published by ATD Press can be purchased by visiting ATD's website at td.org/books or by calling 800.628.2783 or 703.683.8100.

Library of Congress Control Number: 2015938619 (print edition only)

ISBN-10: 1-56286-969-8
ISBN-13: 978-1-56286-969-4
e-ISBN: 978-1-60728-436-9

ATD Press Editorial Staff:
Director: Kristine Luecker
Manager: Christian Green
Community of Practice Manager, Learning & Development: Amanda Smith

Trainers Publishing House (TPH), Fairfax, VA, www.trainerspublishinghouse.com:
Publisher: Cat Russo
Project, Editorial, and Production Management: Jacqueline Edlund-Braun, Editorial Director
Cover and Text Design: Ana Ilieva Foreman/Design
Composition: Kristin Goble, Perfectype, Nashville, TN, and Debra Deysher, Double D Media, Reading, PA
Proofreading and Image Research: Tora Estep
Cover Art: Shutterstock
Presentation Slide Art: Fotolia

Printed by Data Reproductions Corporation, Auburn Hills, MI, www.datarepro.com

The ATD Workshop Series

Whether you are a professional trainer who needs to pull together a new training program next week, or someone who does a bit of training as a part of your job, you'll find the ATD Workshop series is a timesaver.

Topics deliver key learning on today's most pressing business needs, including training for communication skills, leadership, coaching, new supervisors, customer service, new employee orientation, and more. The series is designed for busy training and HR professionals, consultants, and managers who need to deliver training quickly to optimize performance now.

Each ATD Workshop book provides all the content and trainer's tools you need to create and deliver compelling training guaranteed to

- **enhance** learner engagement
- **deepen** learner understanding
- **increase** learning application.

Each book in the series offers innovative and engaging programs designed by leading experts and grounded in design and delivery best practices and theory. It is like having an expert trainer helping you with each step in the workshop process. The straightforward, practical instructions help you prepare and deliver the workshops quickly and effectively. Flexible timing options allow you to choose from half-day, full-day, and two-day workshop formats, or to create your own, using the tips and strategies presented for customizing the workshops to fit your unique business environment. Each ATD Workshop book also comes with guidance on leveraging learning technologies to maximize workshop design and delivery efficiency and access to all the training materials you will need, including activities, handouts, tools, assessments, and presentation slides.

Contents

Foreword

In 2002, we launched the ASTD Trainer's WorkShop Series—a collection of books authored by practitioners that focused on the design and delivery of training on popular soft-skills topics. The creation of this series was a departure for us. These workshops-in-a-book were created to help internal trainers expedite their program delivery by using appropriate and exceptionally designed content that could be adapted and repurposed.

These topics, dealing with issues ranging from customer service to leadership to manager skills, continue to be important training programs offered in companies and organizations of all sizes and across the globe. The ASTD Trainer's WorkShop Series has helped more than 60,000 trainers and occasional trainers deliver top-notch programs that meet business needs and help drive performance.

And while many things about the delivery of soft skills training have not changed in the last decade, there have been advances in technology and its use in training. So, when we began talking about how to refresh this popular series, we knew we needed to incorporate technology and new topics. We also wanted to make sure that the new series was cohesively designed and had input from author-practitioners who are, after all, the heart and soul of this series.

Inside *New Supervisor Training* by Elaine Biech, and each of the other titles in the series, you'll find innovative content and fresh program agendas to simplify your delivery of key training topics. You'll also find consistency among titles, with each presented in a contemporary manner, designed by peers, and reflecting the preferences of training professionals who conduct workshops.

We hope that you find tremendous value in the ATD Workshop Series.

Tony Bingham
President & CEO
Association for Talent Development (ATD)
May 2015

Introduction

How to Use This Book

What's in This Chapter

- Why supervisory development matters
- What you need to know about training
- Estimates of time required
- A broad view of what the book includes

Why Is Developing New Supervisors Important?

New first-line supervisors may be the most inadequately prepared employees for the most important job anywhere in the world!

Why inadequately prepared? New supervisors often come straight from being excellent workers at narrow tasks seldom related to people and go directly to a broad role of supervising numerous people with various skill levels. New supervisors go from doing the work to making sure that the work gets done. They were accountable to their immediate supervisor and are now responsible to their manager *and* their direct reports. Making that transition requires a different set of skills for which they often have not had training, coaching, or practice.

Why the most important job? Research by Gallup (2013) and others suggests that business success and bottom-line profits are directly linked to employee engagement. Everything from absenteeism and turnover to quality and customer satisfaction are remarkably better when employees are engaged. And who is responsible for employees who fail to perform, who are underdeveloped, who have low productivity, and who are disengaged? Supervisors.

Good supervisors know how to recruit, hire, and develop employees to meet organizational goals. They know how to coach employees and create a motivational environment to improve performance. They know how to communicate, reinforce, recognize, deliver feedback, and resolve conflict to retain the best employees. Good supervisors are advocates for employees, liaisons to other departments, change agents, trainers, coaches, and leaders. They plan and organize the work, balancing employee involvement. They budget, delegate, communicate, innovate, motivate, and negotiate.

In short, new supervisors have a lot to learn to be successful in their new role.

Moreover, exit interviews show that people leave jobs because their managers and supervisors don't have the skills and attitudes to keep them happy with the work. It is easy to see why supervisors are critical to organizations. Given the complex mix of roles and responsibilities, it is equally easy to see why many new supervisors may not have the skills they need.

These unsung—and often undertrained—heroes touch many lives and require many skills. So how can organizations begin to develop and prepare new supervisors for these critical roles? The workshops in this book will help you build the skills of new supervisors to prepare them for perhaps the most important jobs in your organization.

The workshop agendas organize the many tasks and roles supervisors have into five key areas:

- promoting communication
- guiding the work
- leading the workforce
- coaching employee performance
- developing themselves.

Learning to be a supervisor is a long journey. No one training program can begin to cover all the details and nuances of the job (for example, we dedicate only one learning activity to delegation skills in the workshop, when authors have written entire books about that topic). The activities and handouts in this book are designed to help you set your new supervisors heading in the right direction.

What Do I Need to Know About Training?

The ATD Workshop Series is designed to be adaptable for many levels of both training facilitation and topic expertise. Circle the answers in the following quick assessment that most closely align with your levels of expertise and your organization's commitment to learning. Each question circled in the column labeled 3 gets three points, and so on. Sum up your total score.

QUICK ASSESSMENT: HOW EXPERT DO I NEED TO BE?			
Question	**3**	**2**	**1**
What is your expertise as a facilitator?	Expert (more than 5 years, always awesome evaluations)	Some experience (1–5 years, sometimes talk too much)	Beginner (less than 1 year, no idea what to do)
How familiar are you with the topic?	Evolving expert (have taken courses, read books, created materials, *and* it is my passion)	Some experience (have taken courses, read books, and created materials)	Beginner (had a course in school)
How committed is your company to investing in training or performance improvement?	Integral part of our corporate culture	Depends on the topic—this one is hot right now	Cheap and fast
TOTAL:			

If you scored 1-3 (novice at both training and topic): Your best bet is to stick closely to the materials as they are designed. Spend extra time with the content to learn as much as possible about it. Also, closely read Chapter 8 on training delivery and consider practicing with a colleague before delivering the program.

If you scored 4-6 (topic expert): Use the outline and materials, but feel free to include materials you have developed and believe are relevant to the topic.

If you scored 7-9 (training expert): Feel free to adapt the agendas and materials as you see fit and use any materials that you have already developed, or simply incorporate training activities, tools, handouts, and so forth into your own agenda.

For more on facilitation skills, see Chapter 8 in this volume. Chapter 12 includes a comprehensive assessment instrument that will help you manage your professional development and increase the effectiveness of your new supervisor training sessions (see Assessment 3: Facilitator Competencies).

How Much Time Will Preparation Take?

Putting together and facilitating a training workshop, even when the agendas, activities, tools, and assessments are created for you, can be time consuming. For planning purposes, estimate about four days of preparation time for a two-day course.

What Are the Important Features of the Book?

Section I includes the various workshop designs (from half-day to two days) with agendas and thumbnails from presentation slides as well as a chapter on customizing the workshop for your circumstances. The chapters included are

- Chapter 1. Two-Day Workshop (15 hours program time) + Agenda + PPT (thumbnails)
- Chapter 2. One-Day Workshop (7.5 hours program time) + Agenda + PPT (thumbnails)
- Chapter 3. Half-Day Workshop (3 to 4 hours program time) + Agenda + PPT (thumbnails)
- Chapter 4. Customizing the New Supervisor Training Workshop.

The workshop chapters include advice, instructions, workshop at-a-glance tables, as well as full program agendas.

Section II is standard from book to book in the ATD Workshop Series as a way to provide a consistent foundation of training principles. This section's chapters follow the ADDIE model—the classic instructional design model named after its steps (analysis, design, development, implementation, and evaluation). The chapters are based on best practices and crafted with input from experienced training practitioners. They are meant to help you get up to speed as quickly as possible. Each chapter includes several additional recurring features to help you understand the concepts and ideas presented. The Bare Minimum gives you the bare bones of what you need to know about the topic. Key Points summarize the most important points of each chapter. What to Do Next guides you to your next action steps. And, finally, the Additional Resources section at the end of each chapter gives you options for further reading to broaden your understanding of training design and delivery. Section II chapters include

- Chapter 5. Identifying Needs for New Supervisor Training
- Chapter 6. Understanding the Foundations of Training Design
- Chapter 7. Leveraging Technology to Maximize and Support Design and Delivery
- Chapter 8. Delivering Your New Supervisor Workshop: Be a Great Facilitator
- Chapter 9. Evaluating Workshop Results.

Section III covers information about post-workshop learning:

- Chapter 10. The Follow-Up Coach

Section IV includes all the supporting documents and online guidance:

- Chapter 11. Learning Activities
- Chapter 12. Assessments
- Chapter 13. Handouts
- Chapter 14. Online Tools and Downloads.

The book includes everything you need to prepare for and deliver your workshop:

- **Agendas,** the heart of the series, are laid out in three columns for ease of delivery. The first column shows the timing, the second gives the presentation slide number and image for quick reference, and the third gives instructions and facilitation notes. These are designed to be straightforward, simple agendas that you can take into the training room and use to stay on track. They include cues on the learning activities, notes about tools or handouts to include, and other important delivery tips. You can download the agendas from the website (see Chapter 14) and print them out for easy use.

- **Learning activities,** which are more detailed than the agendas, cover the objectives of the activity, the time and materials required, the steps involved, variations on the activity in some cases, and wrap-up or debriefing questions or comments.

- **Assessments, handouts, and tools** are the training materials you will provide to learners to support the training program. These can include scorecards for games, instructions, reference materials, samples, self-assessments, and so forth.

- **Presentation media** (PowerPoint slides) are deliberately designed to be simple so that you can customize them for your company and context. They are provided for your convenience. Chapter 7 discusses different forms of technology that you can incorporate into your program, including different types of presentation media.

All the program materials are available for download, customization, and duplication. See Chapter 14 for instructions on how to access the materials.

How Are the Agendas Laid Out?

The following agenda is a sample from the two-day workshop.

Day One: (8:00 a.m. to 4:00 p.m.)

TIMING	SLIDES	ACTIVITIES/NOTES/CONSIDERATIONS
8:00 a.m. (10 min)	Slide 1 ATD Workshop New Supervisor Skills Two-Day Workshop	**Welcome and Introduction** Arrive one hour before the start to ensure the room is set up, equipment works, and materials are arranged for participants. This gives you time to make them feel truly welcomed. Chatting with them builds a trusting relationship and opens them up for learning.
8:10 a.m. (20 min)	Slide 2 Embrace Your New Role So you are a supervisor! •What excites you? •What concerns you?	**Learning Activity 1: Embrace Your New Role** • **Handout 1: Embrace Your New Role** This activity is an icebreaker. It will introduce participants to the content, to each other, and to the action orientation of this workshop. It is meant to be lively and noisy. Follow the instructions in the learning activity.
8:30 a.m. (10 min)	Slide 3 Learning Objectives • Assess your supervisory skills • Promote communication for the department • Guide your department's work • Lead the workforce by investing in development • Coach employee performance • Develop yourself	**Learning Objectives** • **Handout 2: New Supervisor Skills Training Objectives** Review the global objectives of the workshop with the participants. Explain that the session has 30 handouts and 17 experiential activities to help them dive more deeply into the content. Ask if they are looking for something specific. Post their responses on a flipchart page and mention them as you address each. Of course, if the content is not included, say so. If you can, provide other resources, telling them how you can help. (Slide 1 of 2)

TIMING	SLIDES	ACTIVITIES/NOTES/CONSIDERATIONS
	Slide 4 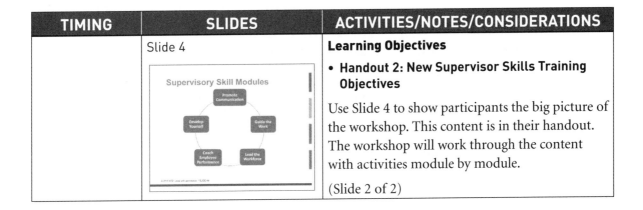	**Learning Objectives** • **Handout 2: New Supervisor Skills Training Objectives** Use Slide 4 to show participants the big picture of the workshop. This content is in their handout. The workshop will work through the content with activities module by module. (Slide 2 of 2)

How Do I Use This Book?

If you've ever read a "Choose Your Own Adventure" book, you will recognize that this book follows a similar principle. Think back to the self-assessment at the beginning of this introduction:

- If you chose *training expert*, you can get right to work preparing one of the workshops in Section I. Use Section II as a reference. Each of the chapters features a sidebar or other information written by the author who has much experience in the topic under consideration. This advice can help guide your preparation, delivery, and evaluation of training.

- If you chose *topic expert*, read Section II in depth and skim the topic content.

- If you chose *novice at training and the topic*, then spend some serious time familiarizing yourself with both Sections I and II.

Once you have a general sense of the material, assemble your workshop. Select the appropriate agenda and then modify the times and training activities as needed and desired. Assemble the materials and familiarize yourself with the topic, the activities, and the presentation media.

Key Points

- Effective supervisor skills help build positive relationships.

- The workshops in this book are designed to be effective at all levels of trainer expertise.

- Good training requires an investment of time.

- The book contains everything you need to create a workshop, including agendas, learning activities, presentation media, assessments, handouts, and tools.

What to Do Next

- Review the agendas presented in Section I and select the best fit for your requirements, time constraints, and budget.

- Based on your level of expertise, skim or read in-depth the chapters in Section II.

- Consider what kind of follow-up learning activities you will want to include with the workshop by reviewing Section III.

Additional Resources

Biech, E. (2008). *10 Steps to Successful Training.* Alexandria, VA: ASTD Press.

Biech, E., ed. (2014). *ASTD Handbook: The Definitive Reference for Training & Development,* 2nd edition. Alexandria, VA: ASTD Press.

Emerson, T., and M. Stewart. (2011). *The Learning and Development Book.* Alexandria, VA: ASTD Press.

Gallup, Inc. (2013). *State of the American Workplace: Employee Engagement Insights for U.S. Business Leaders.* Washington, DC: Gallup.

McCain, D.V., and D.D. Tobey. (2004). *Facilitation Basics.* Alexandria, VA: ASTD Press.

Piskurich, G. (2003). *Trainer Basics.* Alexandria, VA: ASTD Press.

Stolovitch, H.D., and E.J. Keeps. (2011). *Telling Ain't Training,* 2nd edition. Alexandria, VA: ASTD Press.

SECTION I
THE WORKSHOPS

Chapter 1

Two-Day New Supervisor Training Workshop

What's in This Chapter

- Objectives of the two-day New Supervisor Training Workshop
- Summary chart for the flow of content and activities
- Two-day program agenda

Supervisors are on the front line of planning and organizing the work in every organization. Making the leap from worker to supervisor is one of the biggest moves employees make in their careers. Whether you choose a two-day, one-day, half-day, or custom-designed workshop format, time spent on developing supervisory skills will be a solid investment for your organization.

The two-day workshop of course covers more content than the shorter agendas. The longer timeframe enables participants to get to know each other, to build rapport, and to reflect on and practice skills they are learning. They also have a greater opportunity to network with other participants so that they have ready lifelines to call when they return to the job.

A well-designed workshop of any length accounts for and anticipates the natural and predictable "low energy" times during the day, and this is especially true for the two-day program. It is essential to incorporate activities that engage participants, getting them out of their seats and actively participating in relevant and meaningful experiential activities, small group discussion, and practice.

Facilitating a two-day (or longer) workshop requires the facilitator to have a high level of energy and focus and a keen ability to read the energy level of the participants. Keep the participants engaged and the energy high by managing the flow of activities, presentations, personal reflection, and small or large group discussions. The key is variety.

This chapter provides a comprehensive two-day workshop agenda focused on a supervisor's essential areas of responsibility. Making the move from worker to supervisor has the potential to be extremely rewarding or profoundly disappointing. Ensuring that new supervisors are grounded in solid supervisory fundamentals makes a positive difference for the supervisors themselves, for their staff, and for the organization as a whole. New supervisors must learn a plethora of skills to be successful. This workshop bundles together five critical skills areas and allows time for practice plus tips, templates, and checklists to support the learner back on the job. Day one focuses on promoting communication, guiding the work, and leading the workforce. Day two focuses on leading the workforce, coaching employee performance, and continuing to develop as a new supervisor.

Two-Day Workshop Objectives

By the end of the two-day workshop, participants will be able to

- Name five key supervisory skills areas
- Assess their supervisory areas of strength and weakness
- Exhibit communication skills required of supervisors
- Guide work using four management fundamentals to ensure quality completion
- Delegate using a six-step process
- Implement a seven-step process to make decisions and solve problems
- Discuss supervisory essentials of process improvement and change management
- Lead the workforce by hiring the best and investing in employee development
- Coach employee performance to achieve department goals
- Define and model quality and excellence in their departments
- Create a development plan for next steps.

Two-Day Workshop Overview

Day-One Overview

TOPICS	TIMING
Workshop Opening: Embrace Your Role	
Welcome and Introduction	10 minutes
Learning Activity 1: Embrace Your New Role	20 minutes
Learning Objectives	10 minutes
Workshop Guidelines	5 minutes
Learning Activity 2: What's Expected of You	15 minutes
Assessment 1: Essentials of Supervision	35 minutes
Learning Activity 3: Competence, Confidence, and Commitment	25 minutes
BREAK	**15 minutes**
Module I: Promote Communication	
Learning Activity 4: Promote Communication	15 minutes
Learning Activity 5: Share What You Know	60 minutes
Module II: Guide the Work	
Guide the Work—With a 21st-Century Caveat	20 minutes
Morning Debrief: My Most Memorable Morning Remark	10 minutes
LUNCH	**60 minutes**
Learning Activity 6: Eggs-perience a Supervisor's Job	90 minutes
BREAK	**15 minutes**
Learning Activity 6: Eggs-perience a Supervisor's Job	30 minutes
Module III: Lead the Workforce	
Learning Activity 7: What's Engagement Got to Do With It?	35 minutes
Day-One Debrief: My MVT (Most Valuable Tip) of the Day	10 minutes
TOTAL	**480 minutes (8 hours)**

Day-Two Overview

TOPICS	TIMING
Module III: Lead the Workforce (continued)	
Morning Review	15 minutes
Learning Activity 8: Hire the Right Employee	25 minutes
Orient New Employees	10 minutes
Develop Individuals	20 minutes
Learning Activity 9: Foster Teamwork	30 minutes
BREAK	**15 minutes**
Activity 10: It Won't All Be Easy	30 minutes

TOPICS	TIMING
Module IV: Coach Employee Performance	
Learning Activity 11: Establish a Motivating Environment	10 minutes
Five-Step Employee Performance Process	10 minutes
Learning Activity 12: Goals, Roles, and Expectations	15 minutes
Learning Activity 13: Continuous Feedback	15 minutes
Conduct Effective Performance Reviews	10 minutes
Learning Activity 14: Feedback Practice	30 minutes
Negative Feedback Isn't Fun	10 minutes
LUNCH	**60 minutes**
Learning Activity 15: Rewards and Recognition	30 minutes
Retain Your Best	10 minutes
Module V: Develop Yourself	
Learning Activity 16: How Do You Model Excellence?	25 minutes
Manage Your Time	10 minutes
Get Better All the Time	15 minutes
BREAK	**15 minutes**
Learning Activity 17: Develop Your Personal Leadership Guiding Beliefs	30 minutes
Action Planning	20 minutes
Closing: What Do Great Supervisors Do Every Day?	20 minutes
TOTAL	**480 minutes (8 hours)**

Two-Day Workshop Agenda: Day One

The focus of day one is communication, guiding the work, and leading the workforce.

Day One: (8:00 a.m. to 4:00 p.m.)

TIMING	SLIDES	ACTIVITIES/NOTES/CONSIDERATIONS
8:00 a.m. (10 min)	Slide 1 **ATD** Workshop New Supervisor Skills Two-Day Workshop	**Welcome and Introduction** Arrive one hour before the start to ensure the room is set up, equipment works, and materials are arranged for participants. This gives you time to make them feel truly welcomed. Chatting with them builds a trusting relationship and opens them up for learning.

TIMING	SLIDES	ACTIVITIES/NOTES/CONSIDERATIONS
8:10 a.m. (20 min)	Slide 2 Embrace Your New Role So you are a supervisor! •What excites you? •What concerns you?	**Learning Activity 1: Embrace Your New Role** • **Handout 1: Embrace Your New Role** This activity is an icebreaker. It will introduce participants to the content, to each other, and to the action orientation of this workshop. It is meant to be lively and noisy. Follow the instructions in the learning activity.
8:30 a.m. (10 min)	Slide 3 Learning Objectives • Assess your supervisory skills • Promote communication for the department • Guide your department's work • Lead the workforce by investing in development • Coach employee performance • Develop yourself	**Learning Objectives** • **Handout 2: New Supervisor Skills Training Objectives** Review the global objectives of the workshop with the participants. Explain that the session has 30 handouts and 17 experiential activities to help them dive more deeply into the content. Ask if they are looking for something specific. Post their responses on a flipchart page and mention them as you address each. Of course, if the content is not included, say so. If you can, provide other resources, telling them how you can help. (Slide 1 of 2)
	Slide 4 Supervisory Skill Modules Promote Communication Develop Yourself Guide the Work Coach Employee Performance Lead the Workforce	**Learning Objectives** • **Handout 2: New Supervisor Skills Training Objectives** Use Slide 4 to show participants the big picture of the workshop. This content is in their handout. The workshop will work through the content with activities module by module. (Slide 2 of 2)
8:40 a.m. (5 min)	Slide 5 Workshop Guidelines ✓ Start and end on time ✓ Breaks ✓ Ask questions and offer ideas ✓ Get involved ❑ ❑ GROUND RULES	**Workshop Guidelines** Lay out the basic ground rules for the workshop. Ask participants what else they would like to include and add anything you think is pertinent.

TIMING	SLIDES	ACTIVITIES/NOTES/CONSIDERATIONS
8:45 a.m. (15 min)	Slide 6 What's Expected of You **From** •**Your manager?** •**Your employees?** •**Your colleagues?**	**Learning Activity 2: What's Expected of You** • **Handout 3: What's Expected of You** This activity explores the additional responsibilities new supervisors have and how others will expect different things from them. The job title *supervisor* brings with it more accountability than just supervising others. Follow the instructions in the learning activity.
9:00 a.m. (35 min)	Slide 7 Essentials of Supervision **Self-Assessment** •Read each competency and definition. •Rate your skills from 1 to 5. •Take about 20 minutes for assessment. •In which areas are you most skilled? •In which areas do you need most support?	**Assessment 1: Essentials of Supervision** This self-assessment will give your new supervisors another picture of all that is expected of them, this time from one of the most important perspectives—their own! Note that some crossover among the competency definitions exists, not unlike in their new job roles where they will find lots of crossover and very little black and white. I highly recommend that as facilitator you complete the assessment before delivering the workshop to help you prepare for the kinds of questions you will receive.
9:35 a.m. (25 min)	Slide 8 Competence, Confidence, and Commitment **Reflect on what you've heard:** •What skill development will you focus on? •How confident are you feeling? – Why? – What would help? •Are you ready to make a commitment?	**Learning Activity 3: Competence, Confidence, and Commitment** • **Handout 4: Competence, Confidence, and Commitment** This activity helps participants pull together three issues they need to face as new supervisors: 1) What skills will they need? 2) Do they have the confidence (not arrogance) to lead others even if some are older and more experienced than they are? 3) Are they willing to make the commitment that it takes to be the best they can be? Follow the instructions in the learning activity.

TIMING	SLIDES	ACTIVITIES/NOTES/CONSIDERATIONS
10:00 a.m. (15 min)	Slide 9 15-Minute Break	**BREAK** Take time during the break to meet and greet participants who may have arrived late.
10:15 a.m. (15 min)	Slide 10 Promote Communication **You cannot over-communicate.**	**Learning Activity 4: Promote Communication** • **Handout 5: Promote Communication** The sole purpose of this activity is to point to the vital need for new supervisors to communicate, COMMUNICATE, **COMMUNICATE** with their people! Follow the instructions in the learning activity. It is highly recommended that you do not introduce this activity. Just pick up your phone and start the conversation as described in the activity instructions.
10:30 a.m. (60 min)	Slide 11 Share What You Know "More than 60 percent of all management problems are the result of faulty communication." —Peter Drucker	**Learning Activity 5: Share What You Know** • **Handout 6: Share What You Know** As emphasized in the last activity, communication is important, but your participants didn't just fall off a turnip truck. Give them credit for what they already know about communication with this exercise. We all need to be reminded of good communication practices. The debriefing of this activity is very special: Don't miss it. It is 10 times better than going around to each small group for a report. There is a cheat sheet to help you facilitate the debrief—just in case. Use this slide to share the Peter Drucker quote and set up the activity. Follow the instructions in the learning activity. (Slide 1 of 6)

TIMING	SLIDES	ACTIVITIES/NOTES/CONSIDERATIONS
	Slide 12 Share What You Know **Four Basic Communication Areas** •Clear Communication Delivery •Active Listening •Influencing Others Based on Communication Style •Facilitating Effective Meetings **Your Recommendations** **15 minutes**	**Learning Activity 5: Share What You Know** • **Handout 6: Share What You Know** In advance, prepare four flipcharts, place them in four corners of the room, and label each with one of the four basic communication topics: • Clear communication delivery • Active listening • Influencing others based on communication style • Facilitating meetings. Break the participants into four groups and assign each group one of the communication topics. Ask them to review what they know about their assigned topic and to capture their insights on Handout 6 and on their flipchart. Follow the instructions in the learning activity. (Slide 2 of 6)
	Slide 13 Share What You Know **Clear Communication Delivery**	**Learning Activity 5: Share What You Know** • **Handout 6: Share What You Know** After 15 minutes, form new groups by asking everyone to count off by fours. Number flipcharts 1-4 and ask everyone to move to the chart with their corresponding number. Tell participants to move from chart to chart on your signal and repeat exercise at each of the "stations." When all the teams have moved through all four stations, encourage participants to take photos of the final flipchart pages with their smartphones for future use. Note: Slides 13-16 are optional slides. You can use them to guide follow-up discussion or to point out the four topics. If you are using the activity variation with groups presenting their topics to the larger group, use the slides to guide the group through the topics as each team presents. (Slide 3 of 6)

TIMING	SLIDES	ACTIVITIES/NOTES/CONSIDERATIONS
	Slide 14 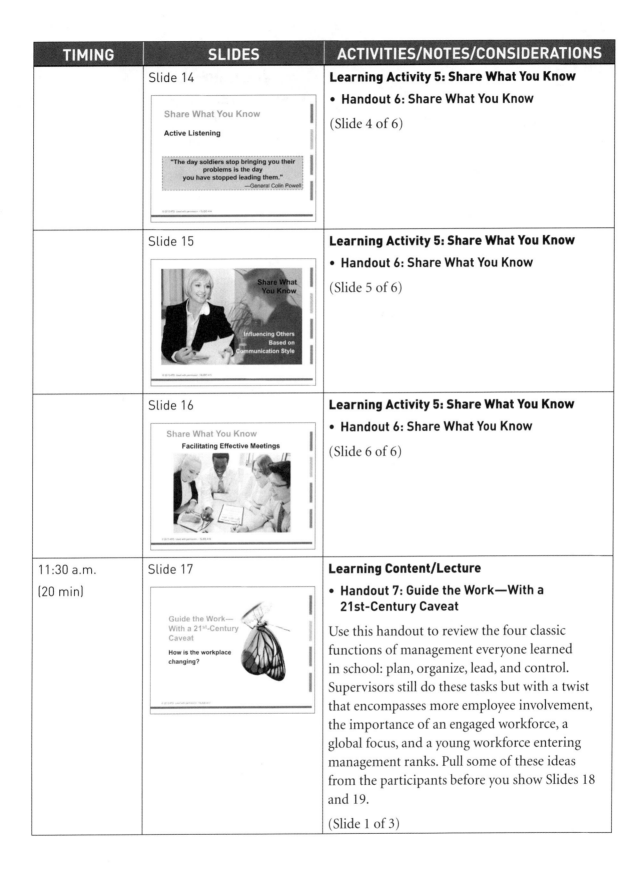 Share What You Know — Active Listening — "The day soldiers stop bringing you their problems is the day you have stopped leading them." —General Colin Powell	**Learning Activity 5: Share What You Know** • **Handout 6: Share What You Know** (Slide 4 of 6)
	Slide 15 — Share What You Know — Influencing Others Based on Communication Style	**Learning Activity 5: Share What You Know** • **Handout 6: Share What You Know** (Slide 5 of 6)
	Slide 16 — Share What You Know — Facilitating Effective Meetings	**Learning Activity 5: Share What You Know** • **Handout 6: Share What You Know** (Slide 6 of 6)
11:30 a.m. (20 min)	Slide 17 — Guide the Work— With a 21st-Century Caveat — How is the workplace changing?	**Learning Content/Lecture** • **Handout 7: Guide the Work—With a 21st-Century Caveat** Use this handout to review the four classic functions of management everyone learned in school: plan, organize, lead, and control. Supervisors still do these tasks but with a twist that encompasses more employee involvement, the importance of an engaged workforce, a global focus, and a young workforce entering management ranks. Pull some of these ideas from the participants before you show Slides 18 and 19. (Slide 1 of 3)

TIMING	SLIDES	ACTIVITIES/NOTES/CONSIDERATIONS
	Slide 18 How Is the Workplace Changing? • Continue to plan, organize, lead, control • More employee involvement • More change • More complexity	**Learning Content/Lecture** • **Handout 7: Guide the Work—With a 21st-Century Caveat** In the changing workplace environment, leaders, including supervisors, will continue to function in the classic management roles. Emphasize that in addition to these functions, they will also be required to tackle more employee involvement, more change, and more complexity. (Slide 2 of 3)
	Slide 19 It's a VUCA World • Volatile • Uncertain • Complex • Ambiguous	**Learning Content/Lecture** • **Handout 7: Guide the Work—With a 21st-Century Caveat** Introduce participants to the VUCA acronym (volatile, uncertain, complex, ambiguous), which attempts to capture the distinctive characteristics of the challenges facing today's workplace. If you aren't familiar with VUCA, you can get yourself up to speed with a quick search on the Internet. Understanding this new environment can help leaders identify and craft responses to meet those challenges more effectively. (Slide 3 of 3)
11:50 a.m. (10 min)	Slide 20 Most Memorable Morning Remark What was the most memorable comment you heard this morning?	**Morning Debrief: My Most Memorable Morning Remark** This activity brings closure to the morning. There are no wrong answers, just an easy, fast-paced review. Keep it moving. Your goal should be to have at least 50 percent of the class offer a comment about something that was memorable to them.
12:00 p.m. (60 min)	Slide 21 Lunch	**LUNCH**

TIMING	SLIDES	ACTIVITIES/NOTES/CONSIDERATIONS
1:00 p.m. (90 min) (Note: Entire activity takes 120 minutes: 90 minutes before the break and 30 minutes after it. You can adjust when you take your break by the amount of time needed to complete team reports.)	Slide 22 Eggs-perience a Supervisor's Job **The ESP Project** •Design a structure — Height of one "strut" — Sturdy enough to hold payload for 10 seconds •15 minutes to plan the prototype •15 minutes to build it •During the planning stage — Plan delegation of responsibilities — Don't touch the building materials	**Learning Activity 6: Eggs-perience a Supervisor's Job** • **Handouts 8a–8d: Eggs-perience a Supervisor's Job** This activity is experiential by design. The participants will all "eggs-perience" several elements of supervising. It is fun and lively and includes a variety of activities and results that create opportunities for learning. The content on the handouts is just enough to get each team headed in the right direction to guarantee learning for all. Follow the instructions in the learning activity. (Slide 1 of 5)
	Slide 23 Eggs-perience a Supervisor's Job **Team Reports** •**Team 1:** 8a, Management Functions •**Team 2:** 8b, Delegation •**Team 3:** 8c & 8d, Decisions, Process Improvement, and Managing Change	**Learning Activity 6: Eggs-perience a Supervisor's Job** • **Handouts 8a–8d: Eggs-perience a Supervisor's Job** Assign each of the teams handouts and topics to complete. See learning activity variations for ideas of how to divide different sized groups into teams. (Slide 2 of 5)
	Slide 24 Eggs-perience a Supervisor's Job Team Reports •Team 1: 8a, Management Functions	**Learning Activity 6: Eggs-perience a Supervisor's Job** • **Handout 8a: Eggs-perience a Supervisor's Job: Management Functions** Tell everyone to turn to Handout 8a. Ask Team 1 to present its report on management functions (10 minutes). Allow for 5 minutes of group discussion after the presentation. Manage the time for the teams. (Slide 3 of 5)

TIMING	SLIDES	ACTIVITIES/NOTES/CONSIDERATIONS
	Slide 25 Eggs-perience a Supervisor's Job **Team Reports** •**Team 2**: 8b, Delegation	**Learning Activity 6: Eggs-perience a Supervisor's Job** • **Handout 8b: Eggs-perience a Supervisor's Job: Delegation** Ask everyone to turn to Handout 8b. Have Team 2 present its report on delegation (10 minutes). Allow for 5 minutes of group discussion after the presentation. Manage the time for the teams. (Slide 4 of 5)
2:30 p.m. (15 min)	Slide 26 15-Minute Break	**BREAK** Pause for a 15-minute break after Teams 1 and 2 present their reports. Team 3 will present its report after the break.
2:45 p.m. (30 min)	Slide 27 Eggs-perience a Supervisor's Job **Team Reports** •**Team 3**: 8c & 8d, Decisions, Process Improvement, and Managing Change	**Learning Activity 6: Eggs-perience a Supervisor's Job** • **Handouts 8c and 8d: Eggs-perience a Supervisor's Job: Decisions, Process Improvement, and Managing Change** Wrap up the activity with Team 3's report. Again, allow 10 minutes for the report and 5 minutes of group discussion. Take 10-15 minutes to debrief the activity as a whole using the questions included in the learning activity. (Slide 5 of 5)
3:15 p.m. (35 min)	Slide 28 What's Engagement Got to Do With It? "All studies, all locations, and all ages agreed that the direct relationship with one's manager is the strongest of all drivers." It's why **YOU** should care.	**Learning Activity 7: What's Engagement Got to Do With It?** • **Handout 9: What's Engagement Got to Do With It?** Use this slide and activity to introduce the topic of engagement. Be sure that everyone leaves this activity understanding the critically important role they play as supervisors in engaging employees and why engaged employees are crucial to organizations' success. Follow the instructions in the learning activity. (Slide 1 of 2)

TIMING	SLIDES	ACTIVITIES/NOTES/CONSIDERATIONS
	Slide 29	**Learning Activity 7: What's Engagement Got to Do With It?** • **Handout 9: What's Engagement Got to Do With It?** Engagement starts with the organization but depends heavily on supervisors, encompassing everything they do. Lead a debrief of the activity by encouraging participants to share their insights and ideas on ways to influence key engagement drivers. (Slide 2 of 2)
3:50 p.m. (10 min)	Slide 30	**Day-One Debrief** **My MVT (Most Valuable Tip) of the Day** This exercise brings closure to the day. Play it up depending upon which sport (MVP) is featured this season. Ask everyone to shout out one idea and encourage them to recognize other participants for ideas too—not just from the workshop materials. You may also want to field questions about day-one topics, share reminders for day two of the workshop, or assign homework (if applicable).

What to Do Between Workshop Days

- Make notes on any questions or follow-up you need to do so you don't forget.
- Capture facilitator lessons learned from the first day of the workshop. Adjust day-two materials if needed.
- Deal with any equipment, room setup, catering, or other learning environment issues you weren't able to address during the workshop.
- Debrief with your co-facilitator, if appropriate.
- Get a good night's sleep so you can arrive early, refreshed, and ready to go for day two.

Two-Day Workshop Agenda: Day Two

The focus of day two is leading the workforce, coaching employee performance, and developing yourself.

TIMING	SLIDES	ACTIVITIES/NOTES/CONSIDERATIONS
8:00 a.m. (15 min)	Slide 31	**Morning Review** Again, arrive early to help your participants feel welcome. Check to ensure that everything is still working properly. Adjust room configuration as needed. (Slide 1 of 2)
	Slide 32	**Morning Review** By way of review, encourage participants to ask any questions they have from yesterday's session. (Slide 2 of 2)
8:15 a.m. (25 min)	Slide 33	**Learning Activity 8: Hire the Right Employee** • **Handout 10: Hire the Right Employee** This activity allows participants to use their mobile devices to learn. It is hoped that when the situation requires "hiring" skills, they will remember to check some of these resources. Follow the instructions in the learning activity.
8:40 a.m. (10 min)	Slide 34	**Learning Content/Lecture** • **Handout 11: Orient New Employees** Orientation isn't an event; it's a process. Briefly discuss orientation with participants, reminding them that as supervisors they have a key role to play in the orientation process. Handout 11 provides a checklist tool to help them assimilate new hires. It is simply meant as a resource for them to use after the session.

TIMING	SLIDES	ACTIVITIES/NOTES/CONSIDERATIONS
8:50 a.m. (20 min)	Slide 35 Develop Individuals You know there are hundreds of methods, such as . . . Tools to help: •Career Goal Questions •Goal Grid •IDPs	**Learning Content/Lecture** • **Handout 12: Develop Individuals** Use Handout 12 to discuss ways to develop employees. This handout will be an excellent resource for participants when they need it. As facilitator, be sure to read it carefully so that you can give a 5-minute presentation about its value to them.
9:10 a.m. (30 min)	Slide 36 Foster Teamwork 3 Teams 3 Questions 3 Teamwork Demonstrations • 10 minutes to plan • 1-5 minutes to present	**Learning Activity 9: Foster Teamwork** • **Handout 13: Foster Teamwork** Establish up front that this activity has no right answers—and that it has no wrong answers either! It is meant to be fun and to show participants how easy it is to identify something that enhances teamwork. Applaud noisily for all the risks each group takes. If this group completed the egg activity on day one, it is appropriate to bring that same group together for this exercise. It will be easier for them to take risks and be creative with a team they already know. Follow the instructions in the learning activity.
9:40 a.m. (15 min)	Slide 37 15-Minute Break	**BREAK**

TIMING	SLIDES	ACTIVITIES/NOTES/CONSIDERATIONS
9:55 a.m. (30 min)	**Slide 38** It Won't All Be Easy **Telecommuters** •Technology •Communication •Accountability	**Learning Activity 10: It Won't All Be Easy** • **Handout 14: It Won't All Be Easy** This activity addresses two issues that commonly present new supervisors with challenges: telework and conflict. Handout 14 introduces three elements for successfully supervising telecommuters. A cheat sheet is provided in the learning activity for you to review before conducting the telecommuter discussion. Follow the instructions in the learning activity. (Slide 1 of 2)
	Slide 39 It Won't All Be Easy **Conflict Resolution** 1.Set the stage 2.Gather information 3.Agree on the problem 4.Brainstorm possible solutions 5.Agree on a solution	**Learning Activity 10: It Won't All Be Easy** • **Handout 14: It Won't All Be Easy** Continue the activity by exploring a five-step process to resolve conflict. Participants will have the opportunity to practice what they learned with a partner exercise. Encourage them to identify their own scenarios for the exercise. (Slide 2 of 2)
10:25 a.m. (10 min)	**Slide 40** Establish a Motivating Environment Reflect on what you do	**Learning Activity 11: Establish a Motivating Environment** • **Handout 15: Establish a Motivating Environment** Use this activity to give participants some time to reflect. Be sure to keep participants quiet for 7 minutes so everyone has an opportunity to think about motivation—or anything else for that matter! Use the last 3 minutes to debrief the activity as a group. Follow the instructions in the learning activity.
10:35 a.m. (10 min)	**Slide 41** Performance: A Five-Step Process **Coaching Employee Performance Cycle** 1.Establish goals, roles, and expectations 2.Give feedback continuously 3.Prepare written performance evaluation 4.Meet with employees 5.Establish new goals and expectations	**Learning Content/Lecture** • **Handout 16: Five-Step Employee Performance Process** Use this handout to introduce the employee performance cycle. There is more detail on this page than most people will need, but first-time supervisors may appreciate it. Emphasize that the most important step in the process is that supervisors provide continuous feedback to help employees grow and learn.

TIMING	SLIDES	ACTIVITIES/NOTES/CONSIDERATIONS
10:45 a.m. (15 min)	Slide 42 **Goals, Roles, and Expectations** Why are goals important? (Step 1 of performance cycle)	**Learning Activity 12: Goals, Roles, and Expectations** • **Handout 17: Goals, Roles, and Expectations** Get your participants out of their seats and jumping for joy about goals—well, not really, but the lesson is essential. Supervisors should encourage employees to set goals—especially stretch goals—to increase productivity. The activity is enjoyable, but don't shortchange the debrief section. They need to remember the lessons too! Follow the instructions in the learning activity.
11:00 a.m. (15 min)	Slide 43 Continuous Feedback **Two Flavors** •Positive for progress •Developmental as learning occurs	**Learning Activity 13: Continuous Feedback** • **Handout 18: Continuous Feedback** This activity will encourage participants to return to their jobs with ideas they can implement immediately to help their employees. Encourage them to check in with their mentor or their manager for other tips and ideas for providing feedback. Follow the instructions in the learning activity.
11:15 a.m. (10 min)	Slide 44 **Effective Performance Reviews** Dos **and** Don'ts •A reference for the future START STOP	**Learning Content/Lecture** • **Handout 19: Conduct Effective Performance Reviews** This handout provides good information when new supervisors conduct their first performance review. They should make a point of knowing where to find the content when the time comes. Briefly review the handout with the participants and encourage them to use it as a resource when they are preparing to conduct performance reviews.
11:25 a.m. (30 min)	Slide 45 Feedback Practice • Select a scenario • Make notes • Work with a partner • Give feedback on the feedback!	**Learning Activity 14: Feedback Practice** • **Handout 20: Feedback Practice** Help the participants practice much of the content covered since the break with this feedback exercise. Be sure to allow the full 30 minutes for this activity. Follow the instructions in the learning activity.

TIMING	SLIDES	ACTIVITIES/NOTES/CONSIDERATIONS
11:55 a.m. (10 min)	Slide 46 Negative Feedback Isn't Fun . . . but we all want it	**Learning Content/Lecture** • **Handout 21: Negative Feedback Isn't Fun** The information on Handout 21 is fascinating. Encourage participants to review the entire blog post at a later time. It seems that we all want to hear more suggestions about how we can improve ourselves. Go figure! That should make it easier for new supervisors to give developmental feedback. Be sure to make this point.
12:05 p.m. (60 min)	Slide 47 Lunch	**LUNCH**
1:05 p.m. (30 min)	Slide 48 Rewards and Recognition When did you feel appreciated?	**Learning Activity 15: Rewards and Recognition** • **Handout 22: Rewards, Recognition, and Retention** This activity comprises two small activities. The first simply points out that people can feel appreciated without additional money—although no one really wants to admit it. The second activity brainstorms a list of rewards that you can use. It also reinforces the importance of goal setting. Follow the instructions in the learning activity.
1:35 p.m. (10 min)	Slide 49 Retain Your Best **Tools for Retention** •Developmental discussions •Stay interviews	**Learning Content/Lecture** • **Handout 23: Retain Your Best** This handout barely scratches the surface of this topic. Briefly review two ideas for increasing retention: development discussions and stay interviews. Emphasize the point that supervisors must begin to recognize their best and brightest and determine how to keep them on board longer.

TIMING	SLIDES	ACTIVITIES/NOTES/CONSIDERATIONS
1:45 p.m. (25 min)	Slide 50 How Do You Model Excellence? **How do you define excellence for** •Your department? •You? **"We are what we repeatedly do. Excellence, then, is not an act, but a habit."** —Aristotle	**Learning Activity 16: How Do You Model Excellence?** • **Handout 24: How Do You Model Excellence?** This activity is the precursor for setting a department vision. The supervisor and the employees need to have a clear picture of what excellence looks like before they can think about envisioning improvements or a better future. Help them see the value in this activity. If you and your participants want to read more about the concept, check out Lisa Haneberg's book, *10 Steps to Be a Successful Manager* (see Handout 30: Reading List for details). Follow the instructions in the learning activity.
2:10 p.m. (10 min)	Slide 51 Develop Yourself: Manage Your Time **Your most precious nonrenewable resource is your time**	**Learning Content/Lecture** • **Handout 25: Manage Your Time** This handout provides a tool that many new supervisors have never used. Time is their most valuable resource. Help them understand that once it is gone, they can never retrieve it again. Lots of resources are available if they want to learn more about time management.
2:20 p.m. (15 min)	Slide 52 Get Better All the Time **What skills do you need to improve?**	**Learning Content/Lecture** • **Handout 26: Get Better All the Time: Your Professional Development** This handout rounds up many ideas for learning. Direct participants to put check marks in front of the content they want to learn more about as well as the methods by which they will learn. Then encourage them to transfer their ideas to their IDP upon returning to their workplace.
2:35 p.m. (15 min)	Slide 53 15-Minute Break	**BREAK**

TIMING	SLIDES	ACTIVITIES/NOTES/CONSIDERATIONS
2:50 p.m. (30 min)	Slide 54 Your Leadership Guiding Beliefs Your role as a supervisor is a turning point in your career: You are "officially" a leader.	**Learning Activity 17: Develop Your Personal Leadership Guiding Beliefs** • **Handout 27: Develop Your Personal Leadership Guiding Beliefs** This is a serious activity. New supervisors need to recognize that they have made the leap into leadership—officially. They need to think about the principles that guide them and whether there is alignment through all parts of their lives. The discussions should be private. You may wish to encourage partners to follow up after the workshop to continue this intensely personal work. Follow the instructions in the learning activity.
3:20 p.m. (20 min)	Slide 55 Action Planning: My Next Steps What? How? When? Who? "People don't plan to fail; they fail to plan." —John Beckley	**Action Planning** • **Handout 28: Action Planning: My Next Steps** The participants don't have time to create an action plan during the workshop, but they can identify what they will do to continue learning. Who can they speak with? Do they have a mentor? Who do they consider their coach and how will that person help them? Walk them through the handout and encourage them to write down their intended actions.

TIMING	SLIDES	ACTIVITIES/NOTES/CONSIDERATIONS
3:40 p.m. (20 min) End 4:00 p.m.	Slide 56 What Do Great Supervisors Do Every Day? As a great supervisor, what will YOU be doing every day?	**Closing: What Do Great Supervisors Do Every Day?** • **Handout 29: What Do Great Supervisors Do Every Day?** • **Handout 30: Reading List (optional)** • **Assessment 2: New Supervisor Training Workshop Evaluation** Close the workshop on a positive note. Distribute the handouts and evaluation form. As participants are completing the evaluation, ask them to think about what they will do *every* day as great supervisors. Gather everyone in a circle and go around asking participants to each share one sentence about what they will do to be effective supervisors. Give everyone a high five and send them on their way to be GREAT supervisors. Be available to field questions about the workshop topics. Share plans for follow-up coaching if applicable (see Chapter 10 for ideas to follow up the training with support and activities).

What to Do Next

- Determine the schedule for training classes; reserve location and catering you may wish to provide.

- Identify and invite participants.

- Inform participants about pre-work such as Assessment 1: Essentials of Supervision, if you are using it in the workshop.

- Review the workshop objectives, activities, and handouts to plan the content you will use.

- Prepare copies of the participant materials and any activity-related materials you may need. Refer to Chapter 14 for information about how to access and use the supplemental materials provided for this workshop.

- Gather tactile items, such as Koosh balls, crayons, magnets, Play-Doh, or others, to place on the tables for tactile learners. See Chapter 8 for other ideas to enhance the learning environment of your workshop.

- Prepare yourself both emotionally and physically. Confirm that you have addressed scheduling and personal concerns so that you can be fully present to facilitate the class.

- Get a good night's sleep before you facilitate your workshop so that you have the energy and focus to deliver an outstanding session for your participants.

Chapter 2

One-Day New Supervisor Training Workshop

What's in This Chapter

- Objectives of the one-day New Supervisor Training Workshop
- Summary chart for the flow of content and activities
- One-day program agenda

There are two approaches you can take to designing and delivering a one-day workshop. You can select one topic and focus only on that topic or you can take a wider perspective and allow the participants to sample a range of topics. Many of the topics in this book lend themselves to full-day discussions, such as time management, delegation, problem solving, engagement, setting goals, and so on, but because of the very nature of a supervisory job, we have chosen the broader approach to the content. The leap from worker to supervisor is one of the biggest moves employees will make in their careers. One of the changes new supervisors must make is learning to think more comprehensively across the organization. Making the thought-process transition from deep and specific to broad and all-inclusive is difficult for many new supervisors.

A supervisor wears many hats and has many responsibilities. Concerns for new supervisors include the larger number of people to whom they are responsible, the larger number of people who have an interest in what they do, and the sheer number of new skills supervisors require compared with an employee with nonsupervisory job responsibilities.

For that reason, this one-day workshop is deliberately designed with a comprehensive overview in mind. In one day participants can explore the myriad responsibilities required of them in their new positions. The one-day session does not try to throw lots of content at the learner. Instead, within the context of the broad job requirements, the workshop allows participants the opportunity to sample multiple job requirements and experience through a scenario how all these responsibilities come together. It gives participants the chance to face how it might actually feel to be bombarded with many requirements at the same time. The accompanying handouts are designed to be excellent sources of information during the training and especially after it ends—to help coach them back at their jobs where they will need it most.

Well-designed workshops incorporate activities that engage participants, getting them out of their seats and actively participating in relevant and meaningful experiential activities, small group discussion, and practice. This workshop offers a good mix of activities, presentations, personal reflection, and small and large group discussions. The key to effective workshops is variety.

Here are some insider thoughts to consider as you prepare for the one-day workshop:

- **A few activity times have been shaved off the two-day agenda.** You will see that timing on a few activities has been shortened, often by only 5 minutes. The two-day workshop provided more time in the design for personal reflection and discussion, which is the ideal situation. However, given the shorter format, we chose shortening an activity over removing it altogether.

- **Several activities have been modified to learning content (handouts) only.** The handouts are excellent resources for participants to use after the workshop. In some cases it might be months before supervisors really need content such as how to conduct a performance review. Rather than skipping the content, we felt it was better to give participants the resources so they will be available when they need them. If you are conducting a series of just-in-time workshops for new supervisors, you may decide to remove the handouts and provide them at a later time. We operated under the assumption that this may be a one-shot opportunity for some new supervisors.

- **Pre-work.** Assessment 1: Essentials of Supervision could be completed as pre-work, which could save 30 minutes in the session, allow time for more discussion, and possibly reduce your feelings of anxiety and angst about rushing. If you have a foolproof way to get everyone to complete it, go for it. Our experience, however, has been that only about a third of participants complete the pre-work and then feel punished while they wait for the other participants to use precious, unplanned workshop time to complete it. The other option is to push full-steam ahead and leave the remaining participants who didn't complete it scrambling to figure out what is going on! Again, your choice.

This chapter provides a comprehensive one-day workshop agenda focused on a supervisor's key areas of responsibility. Making the move from worker to supervisor can be extremely rewarding or profoundly disappointing. Ensuring that new supervisors are grounded in solid supervisory fundamentals makes the positive difference. New supervisors must learn a plethora of skills to be successful. This workshop bundles together critical areas and allows time for practice plus tips, templates, and checklists to support the learner back on the job. The day begins with a skill assessment that points to many other topics the new supervisor should sample along the way to becoming a great supervisor.

One-Day Workshop Objectives

By the end of the one-day workshop, participants will be able to

- Name five key supervisory skills areas
- Assess their supervisory areas of strength and weakness
- Exhibit communication skills required of supervisors
- Guide work using four management fundamentals to ensure quality completion
- Delegate using a six-step process
- Implement a seven-step process to make decisions and solve problems
- Discuss supervisory essentials of process improvement and change management
- Lead the workforce by hiring the best and investing in employee development
- Coach employee performance to achieve department goals
- Determine development plan for next steps.

One-Day Workshop Overview

TOPICS	TIMING
Welcome and Introduction	5 minutes
Learning Activity 1: Embrace Your New Role	20 minutes
Learning Objectives	5 minutes
Workshop Guidelines	5 minutes
Assessment 1: Essentials of Supervision	30 minutes
Learning Activity 4: Promote Communication	20 minutes
Guide the Work—With a 21st-Century Caveat	20 minutes
Hire the Right Employee	10 minutes
BREAK	**15 minutes**
Learning Activity 7: What's Engagement Got to Do With It?	25 minutes

TOPICS	TIMING
Develop Individuals	10 minutes
Learning Activity 11: Establish a Motivating Environment	10 minutes
A Five-Step Employee Performance Process	10 minutes
Goals, Roles, and Expectations	5 minutes
Continuous Feedback	5 minutes
Conduct Effective Performance Reviews	5 minutes
Learning Activity 14: Feedback Practice	30 minutes
Morning Debrief: My Most Memorable Morning Remark	10 minutes
LUNCH	**60 minutes**
Learning Activity 6: Eggs-perience a Supervisor's Job	115 minutes
BREAK	**15 minutes**
Negative Feedback Isn't Fun	5 minutes
Manage Your Time	10 minutes
Action Planning: My Next Steps	15 minutes
Closing: What Do Great Supervisors Do Every Day?	20 minutes
TOTAL	**480 minutes (8 hours)**

One-Day Workshop Agenda

The morning begins with an assessment and introduction to the many roles of a supervisor. The afternoon focuses on an activity that allows participants to experience a supervisor's role and some of the responsibilities and issues that come with it.

One Day: (8:00 a.m. to 4:00 p.m.)

TIMING	SLIDES	ACTIVITIES/NOTES/CONSIDERATIONS
8:00 a.m. (5 min)	Slide 1 ATD Workshop New Supervisor Skills One-Day Workshop	**Welcome and Introduction** Arrive one hour before the start to ensure the room is set up, equipment works, and materials are arranged for participants. This gives you time to make them feel truly welcomed. Chatting with them builds a trusting relationship and opens them up for learning.

TIMING	SLIDES	ACTIVITIES/NOTES/CONSIDERATIONS
8:05 a.m. (20 min)	Slide 2 **Embrace Your New Role** So you are a supervisor! •What excites you? •What concerns you?	**Learning Activity 1: Embrace Your New Role** • **Handout 1: Embrace Your New Role** This activity is an icebreaker. It will introduce participants to the content, to each other, and to the action orientation of this workshop. It is meant to be lively and noisy. Follow the instructions in the learning activity.
8:25 a.m. (5 min)	Slide 3 Learning Objectives • Assess your supervisory skills • Promote communication for the department • Guide your department's work • Lead the workforce by investing in development • Coach employee performance • Develop yourself	**Learning Objectives** • **Handout 2: New Supervisor Skills Training Objectives** Review the global objectives of the workshop with the participants. Explain that the session covers more specific objectives in each activity. The handouts provide more detailed content than listed here. Ask if they are looking for something specific. Post their responses on a flipchart page and mention them as you address each. Of course, if the content is not included, say so. If you can, provide other resources, telling them how you can help. (Slide 1 of 2)
	Slide 4 Supervisory Skill Modules Promote Communication Develop Yourself Guide the Work Coach Employee Performance Lead the Workforce	**Learning Objectives** • **Handout 2: New Supervisor Skills Training Objectives** Use Slide 4 and Handout 2 to show participants the big picture of the workshop. Together, you will work through the content with activities and other resources module by module. (Slide 2 of 2)
8:30 a.m. (5 min)	Slide 5 Workshop Guidelines ✓ Start and end on time ✓ Breaks ✓ Ask questions and offer ideas ✓ Get involved ❑ ❑ GROUND RULES	**Workshop Guidelines** Lay out the basic ground rules for the workshop. Ask participants what else they would like to include and add anything you think is pertinent.

TIMING	SLIDES	ACTIVITIES/NOTES/CONSIDERATIONS
8:35 a.m. (30 min)	Slide 6 Essentials of Supervision **Self-Assessment** •Read each competency and definition. •Rate your skills from 1 to 5. •Take about 20 minutes for assessment. •In which areas are you most skilled? •In which areas do you need most support?	**Assessment 1: Essentials of Supervision** This self-assessment will give your new supervisors another picture of all that is expected of them, this time from one of the most important perspectives—their own! Note that some crossover among the competency definitions exists, not unlike in their new job roles where they will find lots of crossover and very little black and white. I highly recommend that as facilitator you complete the assessment before delivering the workshop to help you prepare for the kinds of questions you will receive.
9:05 a.m. (20 min)	Slide 7 Promote Communication You cannot over-communicate.	**Learning Activity 4: Promote Communication** • **Handout 5: Promote Communication** The sole purpose of this activity is to point to the vital need for new supervisors to communicate, COMMUNICATE, **COMMUNICATE** with their people! Follow the instructions in the learning activity. It is highly recommended that you do not introduce this activity. Just pick up your phone and start the conversation as described in the activity instructions. (Slide 1 of 2)
	Slide 8 Share What You Know "More than 60 percent of all management problems are the result of faulty communication." —Peter Drucker	**Learning Activity 4: Promote Communication** **Handout 5: Promote Communication** Wrap up the activity by sharing the Peter Drucker quote and asking participants to brainstorm what other communication skills are critical for supervisors. (Slide 2 of 2)

TIMING	SLIDES	ACTIVITIES/NOTES/CONSIDERATIONS
9:25 a.m. (20 min)	Slide 9 Guide the Work—With a 21st-Century Caveat **How is the workplace changing?**	**Learning Content/Lecture** • **Handout 7: Guide the Work—With a 21st-Century Caveat** Use this handout to review the four classic functions of management everyone learned in school: plan, organize, lead, and control. Supervisors still do these tasks but with a twist that encompasses more employee involvement, the importance of an engaged workforce, a global focus, and a young workforce entering management ranks. Pull some of these ideas from the participants before you show Slides 10 and 11. (Slide 1 of 3)
	Slide 10 How Is the Workplace Changing? • Continue to plan, organize, lead, control • More employee involvement • More change • More complexity	**Learning Content/Lecture** • **Handout 7: Guide the Work—With a 21st-Century Caveat** In the changing workplace environment, leaders, including supervisors, will continue to function in the classic management roles. Emphasize that in addition to these functions, they will also be required to tackle more employee involvement, more change, and more complexity. (Slide 2 of 3)
	Slide 11 **It's a VUCA World** • Volatile • Uncertain • Complex • Ambiguous	**Learning Content/Lecture** • **Handout 7: Guide the Work—With a 21st-Century Caveat** Introduce participants to the VUCA acronym (volatile, uncertain, complex, ambiguous), which attempts to capture the distinctive characteristics of the challenges facing today's workplace. If you aren't familiar with VUCA, you can get yourself up to speed with a quick search on the Internet. Understanding this new environment can help leaders identify and craft responses to meet those challenges more effectively. (Slide 3 of 3)

TIMING	SLIDES	ACTIVITIES/NOTES/CONSIDERATIONS
9:45 a.m. (10 min)	Slide 12 Hire the Right Employee **Good recruitment page** •What would attract a candidate? •How do you attract a candidate? **Source of excellent interview questions** •Examples	**Learning Content/Lecture** • **Handout 10: Hire the Right Employee** This handout suggests how participants can improve their hiring processes. It is hoped that when the situation requires "hiring" skills, they will reference and use some of these steps.
9:55 a.m. (15 min)	Slide 13 15-Minute Break	**BREAK** Take time during the break to meet and greet participants who may have arrived late.
10:10 a.m. (25 min)	Slide 14 What's Engagement Got to Do With It? "All studies, all locations, and all ages agreed that the direct relationship with one's manager is the strongest of all drivers." It's why **YOU** should care.	**Learning Activity 7: What's Engagement Got to Do With It?** • **Handout 9: What's Engagement Got to Do With It?** Use this slide and activity to introduce the topic of engagement. Be sure that everyone leaves this activity understanding the critically important role they play as supervisors in engaging employees and why engaged employees are crucial to organizations' success. Follow the instructions in the learning activity. (Slide 1 of 2)
	Slide 15 What's Engagement Got to Do With It? I do care . . . What can I do?	**Learning Activity 7: What's Engagement Got to Do With It?** • **Handout 9: What's Engagement Got to Do With It?** Engagement starts with the organization but depends heavily on supervisors, encompassing everything they do. Lead a debrief of the activity by encouraging participants to share their insights and ideas on ways to influence key engagement drivers. (Slide 2 of 2)

TIMING	SLIDES	ACTIVITIES/NOTES/CONSIDERATIONS
10:35 p.m. (10 min)	Slide 16 Develop Individuals You know there are hundreds of methods, such as . . . **Tools to help:** •Career Goal Questions •Goal Grid •IDPs	**Learning Content/Lecture** • **Handout 12: Develop Individuals** Use Handout 12 to discuss ways to develop employees. This handout will be an excellent resource for participants when they need it. As facilitator, be sure to read it carefully so that you can give a 5-minute presentation about its value to them.
10:45 a.m. (10 min)	Slide 17 Establish a Motivating Environment Reflect on what you do MOTIVATION	**Learning Activity 11: Establish a Motivating Environment** • **Handout 15: Establish a Motivating Environment** Use this activity to give participants some time to reflect. Be sure to keep participants quiet for 7 minutes so everyone has an opportunity to think about motivation—or anything else for that matter! Use the last 3 minutes to debrief the activity as a group. Follow the instructions in the learning activity.
10:55 a.m. (10 min)	Slide 18 Performance: A Five-Step Process **Coaching Employee Performance Cycle** 1.Establish goals, roles, and expectations 2.Give feedback continuously 3.Prepare written performance evaluation 4.Meet with employees 5.Establish new goals and expectations	**Learning Content/Lecture** • **Handout 16: Five-Step Employee Performance Process** Use this handout to introduce the employee performance cycle. There is more detail on this page than most people will need, but first-time supervisors may appreciate it. Emphasize that the most important step in the process is that supervisors provide continuous feedback to help employees grow and learn.
11:05 a.m. (5 min)	Slide 19 Goals, Roles, and Expectations Why are goals important? (Step 1 of performance cycle)	**Learning Content/Lecture** • **Handout 17: Goals, Roles, and Expectations** Introduce these next three slides and their accompanying handouts as excellent resources to help support the five-step employee performance process. Use this slide and handout to review the importance of setting goals. Supervisors should encourage employees to set goals—especially stretch goals—to increase productivity.

TIMING	SLIDES	ACTIVITIES/NOTES/CONSIDERATIONS
11:10 a.m. (5 min)	Slide 20 Continuous Feedback **Two Flavors** •Positive for progress •Developmental as learning occurs	**Learning Content/Lecture** • **Handout 18: Continuous Feedback** Handout 18 will help participants return to their jobs with ideas they can implement immediately to help their employees. Encourage them to check in with their mentor or their manager for other tips and ideas for providing feedback.
11:15 a.m. (5 min)	Slide 21 **Effective Performance Reviews** Dos **and** Don'ts •A reference for the future START STOP	**Learning Content/Lecture** • **Handout 19: Conduct Effective Performance Reviews** This handout provides good information when new supervisors conduct their first performance review. They should make a point of knowing where to find the content when the time comes. Briefly review the handout with the participants and encourage them to use it as a resource when they are preparing to conduct performance reviews.
11:20 a.m. (30 min)	Slide 22 Feedback Practice • Select a scenario • Make notes • Work with a partner • Give feedback on the feedback!	**Learning Activity 14: Feedback Practice** • **Handout 20: Feedback Practice** Help the participants practice much of the content covered since the break with this feedback exercise. Be sure to allow the full 30 minutes for this activity. Follow the instructions in the learning activity.
11:50 a.m. (10 min)	Slide 23 Most Memorable Morning Remark **What was the most memorable comment you heard this morning?**	**Morning Debrief: My Most Memorable Morning Remark** This activity brings closure to the morning. There are no wrong answers, just an easy, fast-paced review. Keep it moving. Your goal should be to have at least 50 percent of the class offer a comment about something that was memorable to them.

TIMING	SLIDES	ACTIVITIES/NOTES/CONSIDERATIONS
12:00 p.m. (60 min)	Slide 24 Lunch	**LUNCH**
1:00 p.m. (115 min)	Slide 25 Eggs-perience a Supervisor's Job **The ESP Project** •Design a structure – Height of one "strut" – Sturdy enough to hold payload for 10 seconds •15 minutes to plan the prototype •15 minutes to build it •During the planning stage – Plan delegation of responsibilities – Don't touch the building materials	**Learning Activity 6: Eggs-perience a Supervisor's Job** • **Handouts 8a–8d: Eggs-perience a Supervisor's Job** This activity is experiential by design. The participants will all "eggs-perience" several elements of supervising. It is fun and lively and includes a variety of activities and results that create opportunities for learning. The content on the handouts is just enough to get each team headed in the right direction to guarantee learning for all. Follow the instructions in the learning activity, realizing the time is crunched a bit. The break that follows builds in a time cushion if needed. (Slide 1 of 5)
	Slide 26 Eggs-perience a Supervisor's Job **Team Reports** •**Team 1:** 8a, Management Functions •**Team 2:** 8b, Delegation •**Team 3:** 8c & 8d, Decisions, Process Improvement, and Managing Change	**Learning Activity 6: Eggs-perience a Supervisor's Job** • **Handouts 8a–8d: Eggs-perience a Supervisor's Job** Assign each of the teams handouts and topics to complete. See learning activity variations for ideas of how to divide different sized groups into teams. (Slide 2 of 5)

TIMING	SLIDES	ACTIVITIES/NOTES/CONSIDERATIONS
	Slide 27 	**Learning Activity 6: Eggs-perience a Supervisor's Job** • **Handouts 8a: Eggs-perience a Supervisor's Job: Management Functions** Tell everyone to turn to Handout 8a. Ask Team 1 to present its report on management functions (10 minutes). Allow for 5 minutes of group discussion after the presentation. Manage the time for the teams. (Slide 3 of 5)
	Slide 28 	**Learning Activity 6: Eggs-perience a Supervisor's Job** • **Handout 8b: Eggs-perience a Supervisor's Job: Delegation** Ask everyone to turn to Handout 8b. Have Team 2 present its report on delegation (10 minutes). Allow for 5 minutes of group discussion after the presentation. Manage the time for the teams. (Slide 4 of 5)
	Slide 29 	**Learning Activity 6: Eggs-perience a Supervisor's Job** • **Handouts 8c and 8d: Eggs-perience a Supervisor's Job: Decisions, Process Improvement, and Managing Change** Wrap up the activity with Team 3's report. Again, allow 10 minutes for the report and 5 minutes of group discussion. Take 10-15 minutes to debrief the activity as a whole using the questions included in the learning activity. (Slide 5 of 5)
2:55 p.m. (15 min)	Slide 30 	**BREAK** This break can be used to provide the maximum time for the "eggs-perience" if needed.

TIMING	SLIDES	ACTIVITIES/NOTES/CONSIDERATIONS
3:10 a.m. (5 min)	Slide 31 Negative Feedback Isn't Fun . . . but we all want it	**Learning Content/Lecture** • **Handout 21: Negative Feedback Isn't Fun** The information on Handout 21 is fascinating. Encourage participants to review the entire blog post at a later time. It seems that we all want to hear more suggestions about how we can improve ourselves. Go figure! That should make it easier for new supervisors to give developmental feedback. Be sure to make this point.
3:15 p.m. (10 min)	Slide 32 Develop Yourself: Manage Your Time Your most precious nonrenewable resource is your time	**Learning Content/Lecture** • **Handout 25: Manage Your Time** This handout provides a tool that many new supervisors have never used. Time is their most valuable resource. Help them understand that once it is gone, they can never retrieve it again. Lots of resources are available if they want to learn more about time management.
3:25 p.m. (15 min)	Slide 33 Action Planning: My Next Steps What? How? When? Who? "People don't plan to fail; they fail to plan." —John Beckley	**Action Planning** • **Handout 28: Action Planning: My Next Steps** The participants don't have time to create an action plan during the workshop, but they can identify what they will do to continue learning. Who can they speak with? Do they have a mentor? Who do they consider their coach and how will that person help them? Walk them through the handout and encourage them to write down their intended actions.
3:40 p.m. (20 min) End 4:00 p.m.	Slide 34 What Do Great Supervisors Do Every Day? As a great supervisor, what will YOU be doing every day?	**Closing: What Do Great Supervisors Do Every Day?** • **Handout 29: What Do Great Supervisors Do Every Day?** • **Handout 30: Reading List (optional)** • **Assessment 2: New Supervisor Training Workshop Evaluation** Close the workshop on a positive note. Distribute the handouts and evaluation form. As participants are completing the evaluation, ask them to think about what they will do *every* day as great supervisors.

TIMING	SLIDES	ACTIVITIES/NOTES/CONSIDERATIONS
	Slide 34, *continued*	Gather everyone in a circle and go around asking participants to each share one sentence about what they will do to be effective supervisors. Give everyone a high five and send them on their way to be GREAT supervisors.
		Be available to field questions about the workshop topics. Share plans for follow-up coaching if applicable (see Chapter 10 for ideas to follow up the training with support and activities).

What to Do Next

- Determine the schedule for training classes; reserve location and catering you may wish to provide.

- Identify and invite participants.

- Inform participants about pre-work, such as Assessment 1: Essentials of Supervision, if you are using it in the workshop.

- Review the workshop objectives, activities, and handouts to plan the content you will use.

- Prepare copies of the participant materials and any activity-related materials you may need. Refer to Chapter 14 for information about how to access and use the supplemental materials provided for this workshop.

- Gather tactile items, such as Koosh balls, crayons, magnets, Play-Doh, or others, to place on the tables for tactile learners. See Chapter 8 for other ideas to enhance the learning environment of your workshop.

- Prepare yourself both emotionally and physically. Confirm that you have addressed scheduling and personal concerns so that you can be fully present to facilitate the class.

- Get a good night's sleep before you facilitate your workshop so that you have the energy and focus to deliver an outstanding session for your participants.

Chapter 3

Half-Day
New Supervisor
Training Workshop

What's in This Chapter

- Objectives of the half-day New Supervisor Training Workshop

- Summary chart for the flow of content and activities

- Half-day program agenda

There are two approaches you can take to designing and delivering a half-day workshop. You can select one topic and focus only on that topic or you can take a broader perspective and allow the participants to sample a range of topics such as time management, delegation, problem solving, engagement, setting goals, and others. Because of the very nature of a supervisory job, we have chosen the broader approach to the content. The leap from worker to supervisor is one of the biggest moves employees will make in their careers. New supervisors must learn to think more comprehensively across the organization. Transitioning from deep and specific to broad and all-inclusive is difficult for many new supervisors, and this workshop helps them do just that.

For that reason, the half-day workshop is deliberately designed with a comprehensive overview in mind. Within 30 minutes of the session, participants will take part in a scenario that gives them the chance to experience how it might actually feel to be bombarded with many requirements at the same time. The accompanying handouts provide excellent sources of information to help coach new supervisors back on their jobs where they will need it most.

This workshop incorporates activities that engage participants, getting them out of their seats and actively participating in relevant and meaningful experiential activities, small group discussion, and practice. It presents a good mix of activities, presentations, personal reflection, and small- and large-group discussions. The key is variety.

Here are some insider thoughts to consider as you prepare for your half-day workshop:

- **A few activity times have been shaved off the two-day agenda.** You will see that timing on a few activities has been shortened, often by only 5 minutes. The two-day workshop provided more time in the design for personal reflection and discussion, which is the ideal situation. However, given the shorter format, we chose shortening an activity over removing it altogether.

- **Several activities have been modified to learning content (handouts) only.** The handouts are excellent resources for participants to use after the workshop. In some cases it might be months before supervisors really need content such as how to conduct a performance review. Rather than skipping the content, we felt it was better to give participants the resources so they will be available when they need them. If you are conducting a series of just-in-time workshops for new supervisors, you may decide to remove the handouts and provide them at a later time. We operated under the assumption that this may be a one-shot opportunity for some new supervisors.

- **Pre-work.** If you wanted to include an option for self-assessment as a part of the workshop, you could assign Assessment 1: Essentials of Supervision as pre-work to save time. It is not, however, included in the design of this workshop.

- **Post-work.** Assessment 1 could also be used as a follow-up activity after the workshop. Consider emailing it to the participants after the session. Encourage everyone to complete the assessment and then share their results and which competencies they need to develop with their supervisors and peer partners. Create buddies or use a wiki to post ideas and additional content. See Chapter 10 for follow-up ideas.

This chapter provides a lively half-day workshop agenda focused on a supervisor's key areas of responsibility. Making the move from worker to supervisor can be extremely rewarding or profoundly disappointing. Ensuring that new supervisors are grounded in solid supervisory fundamentals makes the positive difference. New supervisors must learn a plethora of skills to be successful. This workshop bundles together critical areas and allows time for practice plus tips, templates, and checklists to support the learner back on the job. The day begins with an exercise, and topics emanate from it that start the journey of becoming a great supervisor.

Half-Day Workshop Objectives

By the end of the half-day workshop, participants will have resources and knowledge to

- Name five key supervisory skills areas
- Guide work using four management fundamentals
- Delegate using a six-step process
- Implement a seven-step process to make decisions and solve problems
- Discuss supervisory essentials of process improvement and change management
- Coach employee performance
- Determine development plan for next steps.

Half-Day Workshop Overview

TOPICS	TIMING
Welcome and Introduction	5 minutes
Learning Activity 1: Embrace Your New Role	15 minutes
Workshop Guidelines and Objectives	5 minutes
Guide the Work—With a 21st-Century Caveat	10 minutes
Learning Activity 6: Eggs-perience a Supervisor's Job	90 minutes
BREAK	**15 minutes**
Learning Activity 7: What's Engagement Got to Do With It?	20 minutes
Learning Activity 4: Promote Communication	15 minutes
Five-Step Employee Performance Process	10 minutes
Learning Activity 11: Establish a Motivating Environment	10 minutes
Goals, Roles, and Expectations	5 minutes
Continuous Feedback	5 minutes
Conduct Effective Performance Reviews	5 minutes
Action Planning: My Next Steps	10 minutes
Closing: What Do Great Supervisors Do Every Day?	20 minutes
TOTAL	**240 minutes (4 hours)**

Half-Day Workshop Agenda

The session begins with an icebreaker that gets participants talking about what is and isn't good about becoming a supervisor. The heart of the workshop focuses on an activity that allows participants to experience a supervisor's role and some of the responsibilities and issues that come with it. This practical experience opens the door for other discussions and activities focusing on the skills and competencies required to be a great supervisor.

TIMING	SLIDES	ACTIVITIES/NOTES/CONSIDERATIONS
8:00 a.m. (5 min)	Slide 1 ATD Workshop New Supervisor Skills Half-Day Workshop	**Welcome and Introduction** Arrive one hour before the start to ensure the room is set up, equipment works, and materials are arranged for participants. This gives you time to make them feel truly welcomed. Chatting with them builds a trusting relationship and opens them up for learning.
8:05 a.m. (15 min)	Slide 2 Embrace Your New Role So you are a supervisor! •What excites you? •What concerns you?	**Learning Activity 1: Embrace Your New Role** • **Handout 1: Embrace Your New Role** This activity is an icebreaker. It will introduce participants to the content, to each other, and to the action orientation of this workshop. It is meant to be lively and noisy. Follow the instructions in the learning activity.
8:20 a.m. (5 min)	Slide 3 Workshop Guidelines ✓ Start and end on time ✓ Breaks ✓ Ask questions and offer ideas ✓ Get involved ☐ ☐ GROUND RULES	**Workshop Guidelines and Objectives** Lay out the basic ground rules for the workshop. Ask participants what else they would like to include and add anything you think is pertinent. Before the workshop, post the objectives on a flipchart so they are visible during the session. After covering the ground rules, briefly review the objectives with the participants.
8:25 a.m. (10 min)	Slide 4 Guide the Work—With a 21st-Century Caveat How is the workplace changing?	**Learning Content/Lecture** • **Handout 7: Guide the Work—With a 21st-Century Caveat** Use this handout to review the four classic functions of management everyone learned in school: plan, organize, lead, and control. Supervisors still do these tasks but with a twist that encompasses more employee involvement, the importance of an engaged workforce, a global focus, and a young workforce entering management ranks. Pull some of these ideas from the participants before you show Slides 5 and 6. (Slide 1 of 3)

TIMING	SLIDES	ACTIVITIES/NOTES/CONSIDERATIONS
	Slide 5 How Is the Workplace Changing? • Continue to plan, organize, lead, control • More employee involvement • More change • More complexity	**Learning Content/Lecture** • **Handout 7: Guide the Work—With a 21st-Century Caveat** In the changing workplace environment, leaders, including supervisors, will continue to function in the classic management roles. Emphasize that in addition to these functions, they will also be required to tackle more employee involvement, more change, and more complexity. (Slide 2 of 3)
	Slide 6 It's a VUCA World • Volatile • Uncertain • Complex • Ambiguous	**Learning Content/Lecture** • **Handout 7: Guide the Work—With a 21st-Century Caveat** Introduce participants to the VUCA acronym (volatile, uncertain, complex, ambiguous), which attempts to capture the distinctive characteristics of the challenges facing today's workplace. If you aren't familiar with VUCA, you can get yourself up to speed with a quick search on the Internet. Understanding this new environment can help leaders identify and craft responses to meet those challenges more effectively. (Slide 3 of 3)

8:35 a.m.
(90 min)
	Slide 7
	
	Eggs-perience a Supervisor's Job
	The ESP Project
	•Design a structure
	  – Height of one "strut"
	  – Sturdy enough to hold payload for 10 seconds
	•15 minutes to plan the prototype
	•15 minutes to build it
	•During the planning stage
	  – Plan delegation of responsibilities
	  – Don't touch the building materials
		Learning Activity 6: Eggs-perience a Supervisor's Job
		
		• **Handouts 8a–8d: Eggs-perience a Supervisor's Job**
		
		This activity is experiential by design. The participants will all "eggs-perience" several elements of supervising. It is fun and lively and includes a variety of activities and results that create opportunities for learning. The content on the handouts is just enough to get each team headed in the right direction to guarantee learning for all.
		
		Follow the instructions in the learning activity.
		
		(Slide 1 of 5)

TIMING	SLIDES	ACTIVITIES/NOTES/CONSIDERATIONS
	Slide 8 Eggs-perience a Supervisor's Job **Team Reports** •**Team 1:** 8a, Management Functions •**Team 2:** 8b, Delegation •**Team 3:** 8c & 8d, Decisions, Process Improvement, and Managing Change	**Learning Activity 6: Eggs-perience a Supervisor's Job** • **Handouts 8a–8d: Eggs-perience a Supervisor's Job** Assign each of the teams handouts and topics to complete. See learning activity variations for ideas of how to divide different sized groups into teams. (Slide 2 of 5)
	Slide 9 Eggs-perience a Supervisor's Job **Team Reports** •**Team 1:** 8a, Management Functions	**Learning Activity 6: Eggs-perience a Supervisor's Job** • **Handout 8a: Eggs-perience a Supervisor's Job: Management Functions** Tell everyone to turn to Handout 8a. Ask Team 1 to present its report on management functions (10 minutes). Allow for 5 minutes of group discussion after the presentation. Manage the time for the teams. (Slide 3 of 5)
	Slide 10 Eggs-perience a Supervisor's Job **Team Reports** •**Team 2:** 8b, Delegation	**Learning Activity 6: Eggs-perience a Supervisor's Job** • **Handout 8b: Eggs-perience a Supervisor's Job: Delegation** Ask everyone to turn to Handout 8b. Have Team 2 present its report on delegation (10 minutes). Allow for 5 minutes of group discussion after the presentation. Manage the time for the teams. (Slide 4 of 5)
	Slide 11 Eggs-perience a Supervisor's Job **Team Reports** •**Team 3:** 8c & 8d, Decisions, Process Improvement, and Managing Change	**Learning Activity 6: Eggs-perience a Supervisor's Job** • **Handouts 8c and 8d: Eggs-perience a Supervisor's Job: Decisions, Process Improvement, and Managing Change** Wrap up the activity with Team 3's report. Again, allow 10 minutes for the report and 5 minutes of group discussion. Take 10-15 minutes to debrief the activity as a whole using the questions included in the learning activity. (Slide 5 of 5)

TIMING	SLIDES	ACTIVITIES/NOTES/CONSIDERATIONS
10:05 a.m. (15 min)	Slide 12 15-Minute Break	**BREAK** During the break, take time to meet and greet participants who may have arrived late to the session.
10:20 a.m. (20 min)	Slide 13 What's Engagement Got to Do With It? "All studies, all locations, and all ages agreed that the direct relationship with one's manager is the strongest of all drivers." It's why **YOU** should care.	**Learning Activity 7: What's Engagement Got to Do With It?** • **Handout 9: What's Engagement Got to Do With It?** Use this slide and activity to introduce the topic of engagement. Be sure that everyone leaves this activity understanding the critically important role they play as supervisors in engaging employees and why engaged employees are crucial to organizations' success. Follow the instructions in the learning activity. (Slide 1 of 2)
	Slide 14 What's Engagement Got to Do With It? I do care . . . What can I do?	**Learning Activity 7: What's Engagement Got to Do With It?** • **Handout 9: What's Engagement Got to Do With It?** Engagement starts with the organization but depends heavily on supervisors, encompassing everything they do. Lead a debrief of the activity by encouraging participants to share their insights and ideas on ways to influence key engagement drivers. (Slide 2 of 2)

TIMING	SLIDES	ACTIVITIES/NOTES/CONSIDERATIONS
10:40 a.m. (15 min)	Slide 15 Promote Communication You cannot over-communicate.	**Learning Activity 4: Promote Communication** • **Handout 5: Promote Communication** The sole purpose of this activity is to point to the vital need for new supervisors to communicate, COMMUNICATE, **COMMUNICATE** with their people! Follow the instructions in the learning activity. It is highly recommended that you do not introduce this activity. Just pick up your phone and start the conversation as described in the activity instructions. (Slide 1 of 2)
	Slide 16 Share What You Know "More than 60 percent of all management problems are the result of faulty communication." —Peter Drucker	**Learning Activity 4: Promote Communication** • **Handout 5: Promote Communication** Wrap up the activity by sharing the Peter Drucker quote and asking participants to brainstorm what other communication skills are critical for supervisors. (Slide 2 of 2)
10:55 a.m. (10 min)	Slide 17 Performance: A Five-Step Process Coaching Employee Performance Cycle 1. Establish goals, roles, and expectations 2. Give feedback continuously 3. Prepare written performance evaluation 4. Meet with employees 5. Establish new goals and expectations	**Learning Content/Lecture** • **Handout 16: Five-Step Employee Performance Process** Use this handout to introduce the employee performance cycle. There is more detail on this page than most people will need, but first-time supervisors may appreciate it. Emphasize that the most important step in the process is that supervisors provide continuous feedback to help employees grow and learn.

TIMING	SLIDES	ACTIVITIES/NOTES/CONSIDERATIONS
11:05 a.m. (10 min)	Slide 18 Establish a Motivating Environment Reflect on what you do MOTIVATION	**Learning Activity 11: Establish a Motivating Environment** • **Handout 15: Establish a Motivating Environment** Use this activity to give participants some time to reflect. Be sure to keep participants quiet for 7 minutes so everyone has an opportunity to think about motivation—or anything else for that matter! Use the last 3 minutes to debrief the activity as a group. Follow the instructions in the learning activity.
11:15 a.m. (5 min)	Slide 19 Goals, Roles, and Expectations Why are goals important? (Step 1 of performance cycle)	**Learning Content/Lecture** • **Handout 17: Goals, Roles, and Expectations** Introduce these next three slides and handouts as excellent reference resources to support the five-step employee performance process. Review each handout briefly.
11:20 a.m. (5 min)	Slide 20 Continuous Feedback Two Flavors •Positive for progress •Developmental as learning occurs	**Learning Content/Lecture** • **Handout 18: Continuous Feedback** Handout 18 will help participants return to their jobs with ideas they can implement immediately to help their employees. Encourage them to check in with their mentor or their manager for further tips and ideas for providing feedback.
11:25 a.m. (5 min)	Slide 21 Effective Performance Reviews Dos and Don'ts •A reference for the future START STOP	**Learning Content/Lecture** • **Handout 19: Conduct Effective Performance Reviews** This handout provides good information when new supervisors conduct their first performance review. They should make a point of knowing where to find the content when the time comes. Briefly review the handout with the participants and encourage them to use it as a resource when they are preparing to conduct performance reviews.

TIMING	SLIDES	ACTIVITIES/NOTES/CONSIDERATIONS
11:30 a.m. (10 min)	Slide 22 Action Planning: My Next Steps What? How? When? Who? "People don't plan to fail; they fail to plan." —John Beckley	**Action Planning** • **Handout 28: Action Planning: My Next Steps** The participants don't have time to create an action plan during the workshop, but they can identify what they will do to continue learning. Who can they speak with? Do they have a mentor? Who do they consider their coach and how will that person help them? Walk them through the handout and encourage them to write down their intended actions.
11:40 a.m. (20 min) End 12:00 p.m.	Slide 23 What Do Great Supervisors Do Every Day? As a great supervisor, what will YOU be doing every day?	**Closing: What Do Great Supervisors Do Every Day?** • **Handout 29: What Do Great Supervisors Do Every Day?** • **Handout 30: Reading List (optional)** • **Assessment 2: New Supervisor Training Workshop Evaluation** Close the workshop on a positive note. Distribute the handouts and evaluation form. As participants are completing the evaluation, ask them to think about what they will do *every* day as great supervisors. Gather everyone in a circle and go around asking participants to each share one sentence about what they will do to be effective supervisors. Give everyone a high five and send them on their way to be GREAT supervisors. Be available to field questions about the workshop topics. Share plans for follow-up coaching if applicable (see Chapter 10 for ideas to follow up the training with support and activities).

What to Do Next

- Determine the schedule for training classes; reserve location and catering you may wish to provide.

- Identify and invite participants.

- Inform participants about pre-work, such as Assessment 1: Essentials of Supervision, if you will be using pre-work in the workshop.

- Review the workshop objectives, activities, and handouts to plan the content you will use.

- Prepare copies of the participant materials and any activity-related materials you may need. Refer to Chapter 14 for information about how to access and use the supplemental materials provided for this workshop.

- Gather tactile items, such as Koosh balls, crayons, magnets, Play-Doh, or others, you wish to place on the tables for tactile learners. See Chapter 8 for other ideas to enhance the learning environment of your workshop.

- Prepare yourself both emotionally and physically. Confirm that you have addressed scheduling and personal concerns so that you can be fully present to facilitate the class.

- Get a good night's sleep before you facilitate your workshop so that you have the energy and focus to deliver an outstanding session for your participants.

Chapter 4

Customizing the New Supervisor Training Workshop

What's in This Chapter

- Ideas for creating a new supervisor skills series
- Creative approaches for developing lunch-and-learn seminars
- Suggestions for designing theme-based workshops

Many organizations find it difficult to have employees away from the workplace for an entire day or two, even if it is for professional and skill development. As a result you may need to adjust and adapt your workshop to the scheduling needs of the organization. Additionally, organizations often prefer to select the content and topics to match the needs of the employees attending the training. Your training needs analysis will help you prioritize and select the content and activities of highest value for your participants. For more on needs analysis, see Chapter 5 in this volume.

The materials in this ATD Workshop Series volume are designed to meet a variety of training needs. They cover a range of topics related to new supervisor skills training and can be offered in many timeframes and formats. Although lengthy immersion in a learning environment can enhance and increase the depth of learning experiences, the challenges of the workplace sometimes demand that training be done in short, small doses.

By using the expertly designed learning content and activities provided here as a foundation, you can modify and adapt the learning experience by customizing the content and activities, customizing the workshop format, and customizing delivery with technology.

Customizing the Content and Activities

Your level of expertise with training facilitation and supervisory skills will determine how much customization you may want to do. If you are new to both training and the topic, you'll want to stick as closely as possible to the workshop as designed.

If you are a new trainer but an expert in supervision skills, use the outline and materials as designed but feel free to include relevant materials you have developed. If you are an internal training provider, take advantage of any actual documents your organization uses so that your participants practice with content they will use back on the job. The more actual content learners see, the better it will be.

Finally, if you are an expert facilitator, feel free to adapt the agenda and materials as you see necessary. Add new materials that you have developed to augment the learning. Or you can simply incorporate the learning activities, assessments, handouts, and presentation slides into your own agenda.

As you become more confident with both the topic and facilitation, you will be able to introduce more of your own personal style into the workshop. You will also be better able to tailor the workshop to specific organizational needs and business imperatives.

Explore the variations in the learning activities. Many of the learning activities describe ideas for variations to a given activity. Try out some of these alternatives to see which ones resonate with your facilitation style and your participants' preferences.

Customizing the Workshop Format

Use the content from the two-day workshop (Chapter 1) to build a series of two-hour workshops, lunchtime seminars, or thematic workshops.

New Supervisor Skills Series

To address the need to provide learning in shorter segments, Table 4-1 breaks down the content into a series of nine two-hour sessions. These workshops can be offered on a daily, weekly, biweekly, or monthly basis, depending on the scheduling needs of the organization. Note that the segments will require some additional connections to make them a good session. Exploring the topics through additional debriefing questions or adding your organization's documents and examples will make them extremely valuable.

Use Assessment 1: Essentials of Supervision to help participants check off their specific needs while moving through the series.

Table 4-1. New Supervisor Skills Series

SESSION	TWO-HOUR WORKSHOP TOPICS	ACTIVITIES/RESOURCES
1	• Embrace Your New Role • What's Expected of You • Essentials of Supervision Self-Assessment • Competence, Confidence, and Commitment	• Learning Activities 1, 2, 3 • Assessment 1 • Handouts 1, 3, 4
2	• Promote Communication • Share What You Know • Establish a Motivating Environment	• Learning Activities 4, 5, 11 • Handouts 5, 6, 15
3	• Guide the Work—With a 21st-Century Caveat • What's Engagement Got to Do With It? • What Do Great Supervisors Do Every Day?	• Learning Activity 7 • Handouts 7, 9, 29
4	• Eggs-perience a Supervisor's Role	• Learning Activity 6 • Handouts 8a, 8b, 8c, 8d
5	• Hire the Right Employee • Orient New Employees • Develop Individuals • It Won't All Be Easy	• Learning Activities 8, 10 • Handouts 10, 11, 12, 14
6	• Five-Step Employee Performance Process • Goals, Roles, and Expectations • Continuous Feedback • Conduct Effective Performance Reviews	• Learning Activities 12, 13 • Handouts 16, 17, 18, 19
7	• Feedback Practice • Negative Feedback Isn't Fun • My MVT (Most Valuable Tip) of the Day	• Learning Activity 14 • Handouts 20, 21

SESSION	TWO-HOUR WORKSHOP TOPICS	ACTIVITIES/RESOURCES
8	• Rewards and Recognition • Retain Your Best • How Do You Model Excellence?	• Learning Activities 15, 16 • Handouts 22, 23, 24
9	• Foster Teamwork • Manage Your Time • Get Better All the Time • Develop Your Personal Leadership Guiding Beliefs • Action Planning: My Next Steps	• Learning Activities 9, 17 • Handouts 13, 25, 26, 27, 28

Small Bites—Lunch-and-Learn Seminars

Sometimes small means big impact. Table 4-2 shows topics that could be delivered effectively in one-hour sessions. The key to doing these bite-sized chunks successfully is to have a clear design with the right amount of content. Trying to cram in too much content can make a seminar seem shallow and rushed. Ask yourself one question when creating a session of this size: What is the one key concept I would like the participants to remember after this workshop?

Table 4-2. Lunch-and-Learn Seminars

LUNCH-AND-LEARN TOPICS	ACTIVITIES/RESOURCES
• Embrace Your New Role • What's Expected of You • Competence, Confidence, and Commitment	• Learning Activities 1, 2, 3 • Handouts 1, 3, 4
• Essentials of Supervision Self-Assessment	• Assessment 1
• Promote Communication • Establish a Motivating Environment	• Learning Activities 4, 11 • Handouts 5, 15
• Share What You Know	• Learning Activity 5 • Handout 6
• Guide the Work—With a 21st-Century Caveat • Establish a Motivating Environment	• Learning Activity 11 • Handouts 7, 15
• Eggs-perience a Supervisor's Job (through 8a only)	• Learning Activity 6 • Handout 8a
• Eggs-perience a Supervisor's Job (through 8b only) • Retain Your Best	• Learning Activity 6 • Handouts 8b, 23

LUNCH-AND-LEARN TOPICS	ACTIVITIES/RESOURCES
• Five-Step Employee Performance Process • Goals, Roles, and Expectations • Continuous Feedback	• Learning Activities 12, 13 • Handouts 16, 17, 18
• Conduct Effective Performance Reviews • Feedback Practice • Negative Feedback Isn't Fun	• Learning Activity 14 • Handouts 19, 20, 21
• Eggs-perience a Supervisor's Job (through 8c only)	• Learning Activity 6 • Handout 8c
• Hire the Right Employee • Orient New Employees	• Learning Activity 8 • Handouts 10, 11
• Develop Individuals	• Handout 12
• It Won't All Be Easy	• Learning Activity 10 • Handout 14
• How Do You Model Excellence?	• Learning Activity 16 • Handout 24
• Manage Your Time	• Handout 25
• Develop Your Personal Leadership Guiding Beliefs	• Learning Activity 17 • Handout 27
• What's Expected of You • What Do Great Supervisors Do Every Day?	• Learning Activity 2 • Handouts 3, 29
• Book Club: Ask people to read one of the books in Handout 30 and come prepared to discuss it.	• Handout 30

Theme-Based Workshops

Supervision is a broad topic covering many skills and competencies. Often new supervisors are expected to step into a role with multiple responsibilities with very little opportunity to practice. For many new supervisors, their experience is not a gentle glide into a few new responsibilities and expectations but rather a leap into a multitude of difficult situations with complex demands. Table 4-3 shows five major skill themes around which you can create training to help new supervisors: hiring and growing employees, promoting communication, delivering feedback, coaching employee performance, and supervising in the 21st century. This content is developed specifically with "new" supervisors in mind and could be expanded to four or more day-long sessions. Truly a supervisor has much to learn.

Table 4-3. Theme-Based Workshops

THEME	WORKSHOP TOPICS	ACTIVITIES/RESOURCES
Hiring and Growing Employees	• Hire the Right Employee • Orient New Employees • Develop Individuals • Eggs-perience a Supervisor's Job (8b only) • It Won't All Be Easy	• Learning Activities 6, 8, 10 • Handouts 8b, 10, 11, 12, 14
Promoting Communication	• Promote Communication • Share What You Know • Establish a Motivating Environment • Feedback Practice	• Learning Activities 4, 5, 11, 14 • Handouts 5, 6, 15, 20
Delivering Feedback	• Continuous Feedback • Feedback Practice • Negative Feedback Isn't Fun	• Learning Activities 13, 14 • Handouts 18, 20, 21
Coaching Employee Performance	• Five-Step Employee Performance Process • Goals, Roles, and Expectations • Continuous Feedback • Conduct Effective Performance Reviews • Feedback Practice • Negative Feedback Isn't Fun	• Learning Activities 12, 13, 14 • Handouts 16, 17, 18, 19, 20, 21
Supervising in the 21st Century	• Guide the Work—With a 21st-Century Caveat • Eggs-perience a Supervisor's Job (8a only) • What's Engagement Got to Do With It? • Develop Individuals • Establish a Motivating Environment • Retain Your Best	• Learning Activities 6, 7, 11 • Handouts 7, 8a, 9, 12, 15, 23

Customizing Delivery With Technology

Learning technologies can play an important role in adapting workshops to fit your organization. They have the potential to enhance learners' abilities to understand and apply workshop concepts. Examples include webinars, wikis, email groups, online surveys, and teleconferencing, to name just a few. Learn more about how to use technology to maximize learning in Chapter 7 of this book.

The Bare Minimum

With any of these customization options, always keep in mind the essentials of training design (Chapter 6) and delivery (Chapter 8). At a bare minimum, remember these basics:

- **Prepare, prepare, prepare.** Ready the room, the handouts, the equipment, and you. Familiarize yourself with the content, materials, and equipment. Practice can only make you a better facilitator. The more comfortable you feel, the more open and relaxed you will be for your participants. Many things can go wrong: Equipment can fail, the facility can doublebook your room, your Internet connection may not work, or 10 more participants may show up, as you well know. You simply cannot control it all. You can, however, control 100 percent of how much you prepare.

- **Start with a bang.** The beginning of your session is crucial to the dynamics of the workshop. How participants respond to you can set the mood for the remainder of the workshop. Get to the classroom at least an hour before the session begins. Be ready to welcome and greet the participants. Have everything ready so that you are available to learn something about them and their needs. Ask them simple questions to build rapport. After introducing yourself, introduce participants to each other or provide an activity in which participants can meet each other. The more time they spend getting to know you and each other, the more all of you will benefit when the session begins. Once the session starts, conduct an opening ice breaker that introduces the topic, ensures participants learn more about each other, and sets the stage for the rest of the seminar by letting participants know that this will be an active learning session. Try a provocative opening to get their attention.

- **Don't lecture without interaction.** Your learners like to have fun and participate in interactive learning opportunities. Be sure to vary the learning and teaching methods to maintain engagement. Yes, there will be times when you need to deliver information, but be sure to include participants by asking questions, posing critical incidents, incorporating a survey question, or engaging them in a dozen other ways.

- **End strong.** Providing time for participants to reflect and create an action plan at the end of a module or the session will help establish learning. Don't skip this opportunity to encourage participants to take action on something they have learned. Several of the activities in the workshop provide an opportunity to plan for next steps; Handout 15 on establishing a motivating environment, for example, asks participants to identify things that they will start doing to increase employee motivation and engagement. Stress the importance of implementing what they learned upon returning to the workplace.

What to Do Next

- When customizing a workshop it is important to have a clear understanding of the learning objectives. Conduct a needs analysis to identify the gap between what the organization needs and what the employees are able to do and then determine how best to bridge the gap. At the minimum, identify who wants the training, how the results will be defined, why the training is being requested now, and what the budget is. Chapter 5 provides more guidance on identifying training needs.

- Modify or add your own content to an existing agenda from Chapters 1-3 or create your own agenda using the learning support documents included in this book. There is no one way to flow supervision skills content, but you must ensure that the topics build on one another and that you solidly connect the concepts and ideas together to leverage the most of the learning opportunity.

- Make sure to incorporate interactive practice activities into the design of the workshop (Learning Activity 14: Feedback Practice, for example).

- Compile and review all learning activities, handouts, and slides you will use for the session.

- Add your own slides or your own touches to the slides provided.

- Build a detailed plan for preparing for this session, including scheduling and room reservations, invitations, supply list, teaching notes, and time estimates.

SECTION II

ESSENTIALS OF EFFECTIVE NEW SUPERVISOR TRAINING

Chapter 5
Identifying Needs for New Supervisor Training

What's in This Chapter

- Discovering the purpose of needs analysis
- Introducing some data-gathering methods
- Determining the bare minimum needed to deliver training

Ideally, you should always carry out a needs analysis before designing and creating a workshop to address a performance gap. The cost of *not* identifying and carefully considering the performance requirement can be high: wasted training dollars, unhappy staff going to boring or useless sessions, increased disengagement of employees, and so forth. But the world of training is rarely ideal, and the existence of this book, which essentially provides a workshop in a box, is testament to that. This chapter describes the essential theory and techniques for a complete needs analysis to provide the fundamentals of the process and how it fits into designing learning. However, because the decision to train may already be out of your hands, the last part of this chapter provides a bare-bones list of things you need to know to train effectively even if someone just handed you this book and told you to put on a workshop.

Why Needs Analysis?

In short, as a trainer, learning professional, performance consultant, or whatever job title you hold, your role is to ensure that the employees of your organization know how to do the work that will make the organization succeed. That means you must first identify the skills, knowledge, and abilities that the employees need for optimal performance and then determine where these are lacking in the employee population to bridge that gap. However, the most important reason for needs assessment is that it is not your learning experience. You may deliver it, but the learning belongs to the learner. Making decisions for learners about what performance they need without working with them is inappropriate. If you are an experienced facilitator, you have a large repository of PowerPoint decks at your disposal. Resist the urge while talking with your customers to listen for words that allow you to just grab what you already have. Be open to the possibilities. A training needs analysis helps you do this (see Figure 5-1). Methods to identify this information include strategic needs analysis, structured interviews, focus groups, and surveys.

Strategic Needs Analysis

An analysis of future directions usually identifies emerging issues and trends with a major potential effect on a business and its customers over a two- to three-year period. The analysis helps a business develop goals and programs that proactively anticipate and position the organization to influence the future.

Figure 5-1. Introducing the ADDIE Model

A needs analysis is the first step in the classic instructional design model called ADDIE, which is named after its steps: analysis, design, development, implementation, and evaluation. Roughly speaking, the tasks involved in ADDIE are

1. **Analysis:** Gather data about organizational and individual needs as well as the gap between the goals the organization means to accomplish and the skills and knowledge needed to accomplish those goals.

2. **Design:** Identify and plan the topics and sequence of learning to accomplish the desired learning.

3. **Development:** Create the components of the learning event, such as learning activities and materials.

4. **Implementation:** Put on the learning event or launch the learning materials.

5. **Evaluation:** Gather data to determine the outcome of the learning to improve future iterations of the learning, enhance materials and facilitation, and justify budget decisions.

Instructional design models such as ADDIE are a systematic approach to developing learning and could also be viewed as a project management framework for the project phases involved in creating learning events.

A Note from the Author: Getting to Know Participants

Gathering data about your participants is particularly critical for new supervisor workshops. Some of the participants will have no supervising experience at all. Some may have had a forward-thinking supervisor who gave them an opportunity to "supervise" others in a team-lead scenario. Others may have attended basic communication and teamwork classes. And still others may have had a boss who coached them. You will likely have a wide variety of skill levels in the same class.

The purpose of training is to provide participants something that they can apply in the form of skills or knowledge back at the workplace. If your needs assessment questions focus on their past experiences, you will have a clearer idea of how to prepare for the workshop and your participants will have a better chance to gain the skills they will need back on the job.

To conduct such an analysis, organizations look at issues such as expected changes within the business (for example, technology and professional requirements) and expected changes outside the company (for example, the economy, demographics, politics, and the environment).

Results of an analysis provide a rationale for developing company and departmental goals and for making policy and budgetary decisions. From the analysis comes a summary of key change dynamics that will affect the business.

These questions often are asked in strategic needs analysis:

- What information did previous organizational analyses impart?
- Are those issues and trends still relevant?
- Do the results point to what may need to be done differently in the future?
- How has the organization performed in achieving results?
- What is the present workforce like?
- How will it change or need to change?
- What does the organization know about future changes in customer needs?
- Are customer surveys conducted, and if so, what do they reveal?
- How might the organization have to change to serve customers better?
- Is the company's organizational structure working to achieve results?
- What are the strengths and limitations of the company?
- What are the opportunities for positive change?

- What do competitors do or say that might have implications for the organization?
- What are the most important opportunities for the future?
- What are the biggest problems?
- Is the organization in a competitive marketplace?
- How does the organization compare with competitors?

The results can be summarized in a SWOT analysis model (strengths, weaknesses, opportunities, threats—see Figure 5-2). Action plans are then developed to increase the strengths, overcome the weaknesses, plan for the opportunities, and decrease the threats.

Figure 5-2. SWOT Analysis Model

	STRENGTHS	WEAKNESSES
INTERNAL		
	OPPORTUNITIES	THREATS
EXTERNAL		

Structured Interviews

Start structured interviews as high up in the organization as you can go, with the CEO if possible. Make sure that you include input from human resource personnel and line or operations managers and supervisors. Managers and supervisors will want to tell you what they have seen and what they consider the most pressing issues in the organization.

A Note from the Author: Using Social Media for Data Collection

Dr. Kella Price of Price Consulting Group obtains participants' Twitter usernames before the session. If participants don't have Twitter accounts, she provides them with a tutorial prior to the session about how to get one. By using Twitter's online social networking, she is able to ask questions that help her tailor her presentation or content for a learning session.

She tweets each question individually, including the session hashtag in her tweets. She introduces each question with a message such as "I will facilitate next week's training. Pls help tailor training 2ur needs with 5 questions. B sure 2include Q# w/response. #hashtag." Questions might include

- Q1 What is your role and how long have you been a supervisor? #hashtag
- Q2 What do you want to learn as a result of this workshop? #hashtag
- Q3 What skills do you want to gain with this workshop? #hashtag
- Q4 What is your biggest challenge as it relates to supervision? #hashtag
- Q5 How will you use the content in your work? #hashtag

A side benefit of using social media is that the responses stimulate discussion among participants before they arrive in your training session.

Focus Groups

Focus groups can be set up to give people opportunities to brainstorm ideas about issues in the organization and to realize the potential of team involvement. One comment may spark another and so on. Focus groups should begin with questions that you prepare. It is important to record the responses and comments on a flipchart so everyone can see them. If that is not possible, you may simply take notes. Results of the sessions should be compiled.

Surveys

Surveys, whether paper or web based, gather information from a large or geographically dispersed group of employees. The advantages of surveys are speed of data collection, objectivity, repeatability, and ease of analysis.

Individual Learning Needs Analysis

While identifying organizational learning needs is critical to making the best use of an organization's training budget, analyzing individual learning needs is also important. Understanding the training group's current skills and knowledge can help to focus the training on those areas that require most work—this also helps to avoid going over what the individuals already know, thus wasting their time, or losing them by jumping in at too advanced a level. In addition, individual learning needs analysis can uncover unfavorable attitudes about training that trainers will be better able to address if they are prepared for them. For example, some learners may see the training as a waste of time, as an interruption to their normal work, or as a sign of potentially frightening organizational change.

Many of the same methods used to gather data for organizational learning needs are used for individual learning needs analysis. Analyzing employee learning needs should be carried out in a thoughtful, sensitive, and inclusive manner. Here are potential pitfalls to avoid:

- **Don't analyze needs you can't meet.** Training needs analysis raises expectations. It sends a message to employees that the organization expects them to be competent in particular areas.

- **Involve employees directly.** Sometimes employees don't see a value in participating in training. In assessing needs, trainers need to prepare employees to buy into the training. Asking useful questions and listening carefully to stated needs are excellent methods for accomplishing both of those goals. Ask these questions: "To what degree would you like to learn how to do [X] more effectively?" and "To what degree would you seriously consider participating in training to improve your competency in [X]?"

- **Make the identified needs an obvious part of your training design.** Trainees should be able to see that they have influenced the content and emphasis of the training session. A good practice is briefly to summarize the local trends discovered in the training needs analysis when you introduce the goals of the session.

- **Don't think of training as a "magic bullet."** Sometimes a given employee needs coaching, counseling, or consulting, which is best carried out one on one and customized to the individual and the situation. Still other times, the problem is caused by equipment or processes that need upgrading, not people who need training.

The Bare Minimum

As noted, in an ideal world, you would have gathered all this data about the needs of the organization and the employees and determined that training was the right way to connect those dots. However, even if the decision to put on this workshop has already been made, you still need a bare minimum of information to be successful:

- **Who is your project sponsor (who wants to do this, provides the budget, and so on)?** In fact, if you don't have a project sponsor, *stop* the project. Lack of a project sponsor indicates that the project isn't important to the business. Optimally, the project sponsor should come from the business side of the organization. If the project sponsor is the head of training, then the mentality behind the training—"build it and they will come"—is likely wrong. Even compliance training should have a functional sponsor.

- **What does the sponsor want the learners to be able to do when they are done with training?** How does the sponsor define measures of success? Answering these critical questions brings clarity to the sponsor's expectations and thus to the workshop design.

- **What are the objectives of the training?** Use the guideline ABCD to prepare objectives: identify the Audience, describe the Behavior (what will they be able to do that they can't do now), describe the Condition (what are the circumstances under which they need to be able to do the task; for example, will they have a job aid), and then specify to what Degree (level of quality).

- **Why does the sponsor want this right now?** Is something going on in the organization of which you should be aware?

- **What is the budget?** How much time and money will be invested in the training?

Key Points

- Needs analysis identifies the gap between what the organization needs and what the employees are able to do and then determines how best to bridge that gap.

- Methods of data gathering for needs analysis include strategic needs analysis, structured interviews, surveys, focus groups, and others.

- Sometimes, needs analysis is not an option, but some minimum information is necessary, including who wants the training, how the results will be defined, why the training is being requested now, and what the budget is.

What to Do Next

- If you have the option, carry out a needs analysis to determine if this training is really what your organization requires to succeed. If it isn't, prepare to argue against wasting time, money, and effort on training that will not support the organization's goals.

- If you don't have the option of a needs analysis, make sure that you seek out at least the bare minimum information to conduct effective training.

- Prepare the learning objectives using ABCD (identifying audience, behavior, condition, and degree).

- If you have little training background, read the next chapter (Chapter 6) to learn about the theories and concepts that are at the root of training design. If you are an experienced trainer, skim Chapter 6 on design theory or go straight to Chapters 7 and 8 for tips on leveraging technology and delivering training, respectively.

Additional Resources

Biech, E., ed. (2008). *ASTD Handbook for Workplace Learning Professionals.* Alexandria, VA: ASTD Press.

Biech, E., ed. (2014). *ASTD Handbook: The Definitive Reference for Training & Development.* Alexandria, VA: ASTD Press.

Russo, C. "Be a Better Needs Analyst." ASTD *Infoline* no. 258502. Alexandria, VA: ASTD Press.

Tobey, D. (2005). *Needs Assessment Basics.* Alexandria, VA: ASTD Press.

Chapter 6

Understanding the Foundations of Training Design

What's in This Chapter

- Introducing adult learning theory
- Exploring multiple intelligences
- Incorporating whole brain learning
- Learning how theory enters into practice

Because this book provides a fully designed workshop, you don't need to know all the details of designing a course—the design has already been done for you. However, understanding some of the principle design and learning theories that underpin this workshop is useful and helpful—especially if you are somewhat new to the field of workplace training and development. To effectively deliver training to learners requires a core understanding of how and why people learn. This gives you the flexibility to adapt a course to the unique learners in the room as needed.

When designing a workshop, paying attention to content flow is especially important. While there is no one right way to flow new supervisor skills content, you must ensure that the topics build on one another and that you solidly connect the concepts and ideas together so you leverage the most of the learning opportunity. Great supervisor skills require practice, so always include interactive practice sessions in the design of the workshop. Short but well-designed activities can have significant impact.

Basic Adult Learning Theory

The individual trainee addressed in these workshops is typically an adult with learning needs that differ in many (but not all) ways from children. Much has been documented about how adults learn best. A key figure in adult education is Malcolm Knowles, who is often regarded as the father of adult learning. Knowles made several contributions to the field but is best known for popularizing the term *andragogy*, which refers to the art and science of teaching adults. Here are six assumptions about adult learners noted in *The Adult Learner: A Neglected Species* (1984):

- Adults need to know why learning something is important before they learn it.
- Adults have a concept of self and do not like others imposing their will on them.
- Adults have a wealth of knowledge and experience and want that knowledge to be recognized.
- Adults open up to learning when they think that the learning will help them with real problems.
- Adults want to know how the learning will help them in their personal lives.
- Adults respond to external motivations, such as the prospect of a promotion or an increase in salary.

Given these principles of adult learning, designing sessions that are highly interactive and engaging is critical (see sidebar for more tips). Forcing anyone to learn anything is impossible, so the goal of effective training design is to provide every opportunity and encouragement to the potential learner. Involvement of the learner is the key. As an old Chinese proverb says, "Tell me and I will forget. Show me and I may remember. Involve me and I will understand." The designs in this book use several methods to convey information and engage participants. By incorporating varied training media—such as presentation media, discussion sessions, small-group work, structured exercises, and self-assessments—these designs maximize active participant involvement and offer something for every learning style.

In addition to engaging the interest of the learner, interactive training allows you to tap into another source of learning content: the participants themselves. In a group-learning situation, a good learning environment encourages participants to share with others in the group so the entire group's cumulative knowledge can be used.

Tips for Adult Learning

To reach adult learners, incorporate these ideas into your next training session:

- Incorporate self-directed learning activities in the session design.
- Avoid overuse of lectures and "talking to." Emphasize discussion.
- Use interactive methods such as case studies, role playing, and so forth.
- Make the content and materials closely fit assessed needs.
- Allow plenty of time to "process" the learning activities.
- Include applications planning in each learning activity.
- Promote inquiry into problems and affirm the experience of participants.
- Give participants a rationale for becoming involved and provide opportunities for success.
- Promote getting acquainted and interpersonal linkages.
- Diagnose and prioritize learning needs and preferences before and during the session.
- Use learning groups as "home bases" for participants.
- Include interpersonal feedback exercises and opportunities to experiment.
- Use subgroups to provide safety and readiness to engage in open interchange.
- Make all learner assessment self-directed.
- Provide activities that focus on cognitive, affective, and behavioral change.

More Theoretical Ideas Important to Learning

Research on how people learn and how the brain works occurs continuously. A few ideas that come up frequently in training design and delivery are multiple intelligences and whole brain learning.

Multiple Intelligences

Multiple intelligences reflect how people prefer to process information. Howard Gardner, from Harvard University, has been challenging the basic beliefs about intelligence since the early 1980s. Gardner initially described a list of seven intelligences. Later he added three additional intelligences to his list, and he expects the list to continue to grow (Gardner 2011). The intelligences are

- **interpersonal:** aptitude for working with others
- **logical/mathematical:** aptitude for math, logic, and deduction

- **spatial/visual:** aptitude for picturing, seeing
- **musical:** aptitude for musical expression
- **linguistic/verbal:** aptitude for the written and spoken word
- **intrapersonal:** aptitude for working alone
- **bodily kinesthetic:** aptitude for being physical
- **emotional:** aptitude for identifying emotion
- **naturalist:** aptitude for being with nature
- **existential:** aptitude for understanding one's purpose.

How do multiple intelligences affect your learning? Gardner suggests that most people are comfortable in three or four of these intelligences and avoid the others. For example, if you are not comfortable working with other people, doing group case studies may interfere with your ability to process new material. Video-based instruction will not be good for people with lower spatial/visual aptitudes. People with strong bodily/kinesthetic aptitudes prefer to move around while they are learning.

Allowing your learners to use their own strengths and weaknesses helps them process and learn. Here's an example: Suppose you are debriefing one of the exercises in the material. The exercise has been highly interpersonal (team activity), linguistic (lots of talking), spatial/visual (the participants built an object), musical (music was playing), logical/mathematical (there were rules and structure), and kinesthetic (people moved around). You've honored all the processing styles except intrapersonal, so the people who process information in this manner probably need a return to their strength of working alone. Start the debriefing by asking people to quietly work on their own, writing down five observations of the activity. Then ask them to share as a group.

Whole Brain Learning

Ned Herrmann pioneered the concept of whole brain learning in the 1970s, developing the Herrmann Whole Brain Model, which divides the brain into four distinct types of thinking: analytical, sequential, interpersonal, and imaginative. Each individual tends to favor one type of thinking over another, and this thinking preference evolves continually throughout a person's life. In fact, the brain changes all the time with new input and new ways of thinking—a feature that is known as *plasticity*.

Although each person has a preferred thinking style, he or she may prefer it to varying degrees. To identify a person's thinking preference, Herrmann developed the Herrmann Brain Dominance Instrument in 1979. Learning about your own thinking and learning preferences can motivate you to learn new ways to learn and think. For trainers and facilitators, learning about your own preferences can help you identify where you may be neglecting other styles or preferences in your training design and delivery. As Ann Herrmann-Nehdi, daughter of Ned Herrmann and researcher in her own right, notes in the *ASTD Handbook for Workplace Learning Professionals*, "Effective learning is whole brained—designing, delivering, and evaluating the learning to best meet the varying needs of diverse learners" (2008, p. 215).

Herrmann-Nehdi continues, "Our knowledge of the brain and its inherent uniqueness shows that each individual is a unique learner with learning experiences, preferences, and avoidances that will be different from those of other learners. This means that learning designs must somehow factor in the uniqueness of the individual learner" (2008, p. 221). That is to say that effective facilitation must provide a blend of learning activities that addresses various thinking processes from analytical to sequential to interpersonal to imaginative. Because each individual has a unique combination of varying preferences for different types of learning, such a blend can engage most learners even when they are not directly learning in their preferred style. Engaging varied thinking styles ensures *whole brain learning,* rather than a narrow focus on one or two thinking styles.

Here are some tips for incorporating whole brain learning into your facilitation:

- Identify your own thinking preferences to avoid getting too one-sided in your presentation. Deliberately include styles you don't typically prefer.

- Recognize that your learners have unique brains that have continually changed as a result of a lifetime of experiences, learning, and ways of thinking.

- Address those variations in learning and thinking preferences by learning different ways to deliver learning, including facts, case studies, metaphors, brainstorming, simulations, quizzes, outlines, procedures, group learning, role plays, and so on to engage their whole brains.

- Avoid diminishing learners' motivation to learn.

- Avoid overwhelming the brain or causing stress. Stick to need-to-know rather than nice-to-know.

Theory Into Practice

These theories (and more that are not addressed here) affect the way the content of the workshop is put together. Some examples of training features that derive from these theories include handouts, research references, and presentation media to read; quiet time to write notes and reflect; opportunities for listening and talking; and exercises for practicing skills. The workshop activities and materials for the programs in this book have taken these theories to heart in their design, providing content, activities, and tools that will appeal to and engage many learning and thinking styles. Additional ways to translate learning and design theory into practice include the following:

Establishing a Framework

For learners to understand the goals of training and how material relates to real work situations, a framework can be helpful. When presenting the training in the context of a framework, trainers should provide an overview of why the organization has decided to undertake the training and why it is important. This explanation should also highlight what the trainer hopes to accomplish and how the skills learned in this training will be useful back on the job.

Objectives and goals of the programs and learning activities are described in this workbook; share those objectives with the learners when discussing the purposes of specific exercises. Handouts will also help provide a framework for participants.

Identifying Behaviors

Within any training goal are many behaviors. For example, listening and giving clear directions are necessary behaviors for good customer service. Customer service does not improve simply because employees are told to do so—participants need to understand the reasons and see the relevant parts of the equation. For these reasons, facilitators should identify and discuss relevant behaviors throughout the program.

Training helps people identify the behaviors that are important, so that those behaviors can be targeted for improvement. Learning activities enable participants to analyze different skills and behaviors and to separate the parts from the whole. The learning activities in this book, with their clearly stated objectives, have been carefully crafted to take these considerations into account.

Practicing

Practice is crucial for learning because learning takes place by doing and by seeing. In the training designs included in this workbook, practice occurs in written exercises, verbal exercises, and role playing. Role playing helps participants actually practice the behaviors that are being addressed. Role-play exercises bring skills and behaviors to life for those acting out particular roles and for those observing the scenarios.

Learning a new skill takes a lot of practice. Some participants learn skills more quickly than others. Some people's attitudes might prevent them from being open to trying new behaviors.

Your job is to facilitate the session to the best of your ability, taking different learning styles into account. The rest is up to the participants.

Providing Feedback

A key aspect of training is the feedback trainers give to participants. If delivered in a supportive and constructive manner, feedback helps learners develop a deeper understanding of the content you are presenting and the behaviors they are practicing. Feedback in role plays is especially powerful because this is where "the rubber hits the road." In role plays, observers can see if people are able to practice the behaviors that have been discussed, or whether habitual responses will prevail.

Making It Relevant

Throughout the program you will discuss how to use skills and new behaviors on the job. These discussions will help answer the question "So what?" Exercises and action plans help participants bring new skills back to actual work situations. This is also important in addressing the adult need for relevancy in learning.

The Bare Minimum

- **Keep the focus on self-reflection.** Be purposeful in designing content that encourages participants to analyze their own behaviors instead of what others do wrong.
- **Build practice into the design.** As with many skills, supervising improves with practice. Provide your participants with hands-on, engaging opportunities to practice the correct skills.

Key Points

- Adults have specific learning needs that must be addressed in training to make it successful.
- People also have different intelligences; that is, different areas in which they are more comfortable and competent. Addressing different intelligences in the workshop keeps more people engaged in more ways.
- People take in new information in different ways; addressing a variety of different thinking styles can help everyone learn more effectively.
- Bring theory into practice by creating a framework, identifying behaviors, practicing, providing feedback, and making the learning relevant.

What to Do Next

- Look through the training materials to identify how they address the learning theories presented in this book. If you make modifications to the material, consider whether those modifications leave out an intelligence or a thinking style. Can you address more intelligences without making the material cumbersome?

- Read the next chapter to identify how to incorporate technology into the workshop to make it more effective.

Additional Resources

Biech, E., ed. (2008). *ASTD Handbook for Workplace Learning Professionals.* Alexandria, VA: ASTD Press.

Biech, E., ed. (2014). *ASTD Handbook: The Definitive Reference for Training & Development,* 2nd edition. Alexandria, VA: ASTD Press.

Gardner, H. (2006). *Multiple Intelligences: New Horizons in Theory and Practice.* New York: Basic Books.

Gardner, H. (2011). *Frames of Mind: The Theory of Multiple Intelligences.* New York: Basic Books.

Herrmann, N. (1988). *Creative Brain.* Lake Lure, NC: Brain Books.

Herrmann, N. (1996). *Whole Brain Business Book.* San Francisco: McGraw-Hill.

Herrmann-Nehdi, A. (2008). "The Learner: What We Need to Know." In E. Biech, ed., *ASTD Handbook for Workplace Learning Professionals.* Alexandria, VA: ASTD Press.

Jones, J.E., W.L. Bearley, and D.C. Watsabaugh. (1996). *The New Fieldbook for Trainers: Tips, Tools, and Techniques.* Amherst, MA: HRD Press.

Knowles, M.S. (1984). *The Adult Learner: A Neglected Species.* Houston, TX: Gulf Publishing.

Russell, L. (1999). *The Accelerated Learning Fieldbook: Making the Instructional Process Fast, Flexible, and Fun.* San Francisco: Jossey-Bass/Pfeiffer.

Chapter 7

Leveraging Technology to Maximize and Support Design and Delivery

What's in This Chapter

- Recognizing the importance of technology tools

- Determining when to use learning technologies

- Identifying types of learning technologies

- Enhancing learner engagement

- Deepening learner understanding

- Increasing learning application

The workshops offered in this book are designed to be facilitated in person. Even so, learning technologies can and should play a role in adapting workshops to fit your organization, reinforce learning, and measure effectiveness. Technology is an important learning component, but it can also become an expensive distraction. The key is whether and how well technology enhances learners' abilities to understand and apply workshop concepts.

Your use of technology should also align with your organization's culture and readiness. For example, using webinars and wikis in a high-tech environment where employees are familiar with these tools may be logical and welcome, but you might need to introduce these tools more slowly at another company where email is the primary technology used for communication (see Figure 7-1 for some dos and don'ts of recording webinars).

The most important factor to consider when deciding whether to use learning technologies is how they can best support your workshop's learning objectives. This is particularly critical (and not at all straightforward) when delivering this workshop's soft skills training because personal and interpersonal habits and skills tend to require participants to challenge their beliefs and shift their mindsets. This deeper level of self-reflection, though tougher to do in a virtual setting, can be done if you select the right tool and use it at the right time in the learning process.

In the previous chapter, you learned about the adult learning theories and learning styles that underpin the workshops in this volume. Keep these in mind as you assess and weigh opportunities to use learning technologies. In this chapter, you will explore where technology can augment learning transfer and application in your workshop. Please note that the information has been kept general for two reasons. First, each organization has access to specific and limited technologies, and you should learn about them and creatively use what you have. Second, recommendations for specific technologies are likely to become obsolete quickly; so instead, let's focus on the types of learning technologies that might best augment in-person workshops.

Figure 7-1. Dos and Don'ts of Recording Webinars

To increase your chances of a successful webinar, consider and incorporate these tips.

Do
- Introduce yourself and the topic.
- Keep recorded webinars short—ideally 20 minutes or less.
- Use a conversational voice to increase interest.
- Use adequate numbers of slides so that you do not stay on one slide for more than 30 or 45 seconds.
- Address simple, focused topics with five or fewer key points.
- Use pictures and minimal text on slides.

Don't
- Use your computer's microphone to record; instead, invest in a good headset.
- Use a recorded webinar that has poor audio quality; instead, re-record if needed.
- Use too much text or small fonts.
- Assume that participants are just watching the webinar; you have to keep their interest or they will get distracted.
- Try to cover a complex topic using a recorded webinar; the webinar should be focused on one topic with a few main points.

Why Consider Learning Technologies?

You have decided to provide in-person workshops and will use the agendas offered in this book to plan and conduct the training. Learning technologies can be essential tools in your tool kit. Most learning does not occur in the classroom. The workshop is important, but it must be supported by strong pre- and post-course reinforcement. To learn something, learners need many points of contact with the new skills and concepts, such as presentation, reflection, discussion, practice, feedback, and exploration. Moreover, most of your participants are very busy and unable to attend multiple in-person pre- or post-course sessions. So to ensure learning transfer, you can augment in-person activities with technology-based engagement. The good news is that you can use technology in many ways to enhance learning, even of soft skills.

Opportunities to Use Learning Technologies

Whether you have many or few technology resources upon which to draw for learning, start by asking yourself this question: For this topic or series, how can I best use technology to increase learner engagement, understanding, and application? You will use these criteria to discover and evaluate potential ways technology might provide value in the learning process, including

- when designing the training
- before the training
- during the training
- after the training
- while building a learner community.

Note that this chapter offers ways to use technology to enhance traditional learning workshops (blended learning). We assume you will be consulting with a technology partner if you are considering a technology-driven training program—such as a workplace simulation or self-directed online learning. That said, the content found in this training series could be adapted for use in an online learning platform. For more information on how to use the online tools and downloads, see Chapter 14.

When Designing Training

The ATD Workshop Series offers fully designed training you can use with minimal preparation and solid facilitation skills. Even so, you will be creating a learning implementation plan that is an important part of the design process.

A Note from the Author: m-Learning

Learning in the palm of your hand. What could be better? The concept of m-Learning is so new that the profession has yet to agree on a definition. Consider for this discussion that it is learning that occurs through a mobile device such as a smartphone or tablet. Smartphones are used for many things, but not all them can be called "learning."

m-Learning allows you to pair a tiny but critical (either timeframe or importance) data point with a skill check, giving you a quick connection with your learners. And this connection accomplishes several goals: It provides the learner with content, allows the learner to provide you with an update, and keeps the relationship between the two of you alive.

Many conversations about m-Learning focus on "bring your own device" (BYOD, for short), but as a trainer you need to focus on what an effective learning module looks like on a mobile device:

- It is concise—probably less than 5 minutes long.
- It encourages a response from the learner.
- It is straightforward and easy to understand because the user will not likely be in a distraction-free environment.
- It offers support or knowledge required just in time, such as an updated policy, a job aid, or a short communication skill.

A good rule of thumb is to design for the tiniest size screen your new supervisors will be reading on and remember they may likely be distracted when they first see your module.

Here are a few simple examples of how you can use m-Learning for new supervisors:

- Follow up the workshop with a series of mini-modules that act as reminders for some of the new skills presented in your workshop.
- Create "next steps" content. For example, you may have discussed delegation in the workshop but not what happens if someone refuses a task a supervisor is delegating. You could create a mini-module titled "What to do if your employee refuses a delegated task."
- If you know that performance appraisal time will be arriving soon, share a short check list with your participants to remind them of what to do.

The beauty of each of these examples is that once you have designed them, you can use them over and over.

To increase engagement: You have to know your audience members to engage them, because engagement is a choice driven by interest, challenge, and relevance of the topic. Use learning technologies to ensure that you understand where your audience is coming from and the learning approaches they will most value. Email groups, online surveys, teleconferencing, and web meetings with polling can help you ascertain their wants and needs before you solidify your training plan.

To deepen understanding: When in the planning stage, make sure that you have not tried to cram too much presentation into the learning process and that you have planned sufficient time and attention to engaging participants. Flowcharting or mind-mapping software can help you visualize and communicate your learning plan and ensure that you allow for maximum engagement and practice.

To increase application: Increasing retention and application requires buy-in from sponsors and managers to ensure that what is learned is welcomed and applied on the job. Use email groups, online surveys, teleconferencing, and web meetings with polling to communicate with sponsors and managers about what they want out of the training and to identify ways to apply the learning back on the job. Having this information is also valuable in developing the training plan.

Before Training

You want to prime your participants' minds for the topic you will be presenting during the workshop. Pre-work does not have to be something arduous and unwelcome. In fact, a great pre-work assignment can help maximize precious time in the classroom and allow you to focus on the topics that require thorough discussion.

To increase engagement: Tap into the most fascinating aspects of the workshop topic and introduce these through video clips, blog posts, and online resources (see Figure 7-2 about the legal use of video clips, images, and so forth). Avoid boring participants with long "how-to" articles or book chapters before the workshop. In fact, do the opposite and ensure that the pre-work is interesting, provocative (even controversial), and brief. You might select a blog post or video clip that offers a counterpoint to the training or something that inspires your participants to think about the topic before attending training.

To deepen understanding: If you know that the workshop topic will be challenging to some of your participants, prepare and share a brief recorded webinar, video clip, or article that introduces the topic. For example, if your managers tend to tell versus coach, try sharing one or two external resources that discuss the value of service-oriented coaching conversations.

Figure 7-2. Copyright Beware

Copyright law is a sticky, complex area that is beyond the scope of this book to address in detail. For legal advice, consult your legal department.

However, it's very important to note a few things about copyright, fair use, and intellectual property:

- Just because you found an image, article, music, or video online doesn't mean that you can use it in training without permission. Make sure you obtain permission from the copyright owner before you use it (sometimes the copyright owner is not obvious and you will need to do some research).

- Fair use is pretty limited. Although most fair use allows an educational exception, that does *not* include corporate or organizational training. Other exceptions relate to how much material relative to the original was used, the nature of the original work (creative work generally has more protection), and the effect on the market for the original (Swindling and Partridge 2008). Once again, your best bet is to get written permission.

- Just because something doesn't have a copyright notice on it doesn't mean that it isn't copyright protected. All original material is protected under copyright law as soon as it is published or created.

Don't despair. Plenty of online sources of images, videos, text, and so forth exist that you can use for free or for a minimal fee. Just search on the terms "copyright free" or "open source." Another place to look is Wikimedia Commons, which has millions of freely usable media files. For more information about how copyright law affects your use of materials in this volume, please see Chapter 14 on how to use the online materials and downloads.

To increase application: You can improve the chances that your participants will apply what they learn by ensuring they identify real-world work challenges in which they can apply their new skills. Start with a one- or two-question pre-workshop survey (using Survey Monkey or similar) that requires they identify these opportunities and then use the responses to enhance your in-workshop discussions. If your organization has an internal social network or ways to create collaboration groups, use the pre-work questions to begin an online discussion of the topic. The conversations will help your participants think about the topic and will help you prepare for a great workshop (and will give you a beneficial "heads-up" on potential areas of conflict or disagreement).

During Training

Learning technologies can help make your workshops more interesting and can help enhance understanding of the material. Beware, however, that you always want to have a "Plan B" in case of technology glitches or breakdowns. Another critical point to make here is that technology does not change how people learn. Learning and performance drive the technology choice, not the other way around.

To increase engagement: The perennial favorite technology for spicing up a workshop is the use of a great video. Boring videos don't help! If you can find short video clips that reinforce your most important points, please do so. In addition to adding contrast to the workshop flow, having other "experts" say what you want participants to hear is helpful. Another way to increase engagement is to use some kind of audience-response system or electronic polling. Although this might not be practical for small groups (the technology can be a bit pricey), some less expensive alternatives use texting schemas you might want to check out. Your participants will love seeing their collective responses instantly populate your PowerPoint charts. (For more on PowerPoint, see Figure 7-3 and Chapter 8.)

To deepen understanding: Videos can also help improve understanding. If your participants have access to computers during the workshop, consider short technology-based games and short simulations that reinforce the points. You can also ask participants to fill out worksheets and surveys online during the class. Share animated models, flowcharts, or mind maps to help explain key concepts or how they connect together.

To increase application: Learning simulations and practice sessions help prepare participants to apply new skills. You can do these in person, and you can use technology to facilitate practices. This depends a lot on the topic.

After Training

Your participants are busy, and the new skills and concepts they learned in the workshop will become a distant memory without follow-up. Just as you did before the training, you can and should use learning technologies to augment the learning that occurs during the workshop.

Figure 7-3. PowerPoint or Prezi or Other?

Although PowerPoint is the most common presentation software, other platforms you might want to consider include Prezi, GoAnimate, Google Docs, mind-mapping programs, or others. Here are a few key considerations that will help you choose:

- Aside from the in-class workshop, where will you want to share the presentation?
- If you will be sharing the presentation with others, consider whether new software will be required.
- Which presentation platform is best for the content you are presenting, or does it matter?
- What are the costs and resources required for each platform?
- Which platform will partner well with technology tools you will use to reinforce the learning?
- What might be the advantage of using two or more platforms throughout the learning process?

To increase engagement: Learners engage when they perceive something as interesting, relevant right now, or challenging. Use tools such as video, blogs, social networks, chat, websites, and email to increase interest in the topic and to provide challenge.

To deepen understanding: Use post-workshop surveys and polling tools to assess understanding so you can address any gap. Add to the participants' understanding of the topic by posting materials on a SharePoint site or through blog posts that you push to their email inboxes using an RSS feed.

To increase application: Provide a just-in-time online resource where participants find quick reference sheets and get application tips using a group site, social network, or SharePoint site. Request or require that participants report how they have used new skills through an online project management collaboration site, wiki, or email group.

While Building a Learning Community

Creating an ongoing network of learners is extremely valuable, especially for soft skills. The in-person workshop is just the beginning of the learning journey and so keeping learners engaged is helpful. In addition, you want to create a safe place where learners can discuss challenges, provide encouragement, and share their best practices. Learning technologies are particularly useful for building community among learners and teams.

To increase engagement: Busy people value community but often can't make the time to attend follow-up sessions or network with peers. They might, however, be able to take 10 minutes to check in on an internal social network, group site, or blog to learn from and share with others. If your organization does not have social networking or collaboration software, you might need to get creative. Talk to your technology department about the tools you do have—whether they are SharePoint, blog software, internal messaging, a wiki-type project management collaboration tool, or other. You can even use email groups to connect learners. Look for ways you can create pull (they choose when to engage) and push (they get updates), such as using RSS feeds.

To deepen understanding: After the workshop, use web meetings, teleconferencing, and messaging to connect learning partners or mentors and facilitate their sharing real-time application stories. Periodically facilitate online discussion groups to reinforce the learning and bring participants back together.

To increase application: Use a collaborative online project site or social network to set expectations about post-workshop peer discussions and reinforce engagement. Poll participants and assign sub-teams to lead a portion of each web meeting.

The Bare Minimum

- **Know what resources you have available.** Many organizations have widely varying resources; don't assume that you know everything that is available.

- **Stretch yourself.** Be willing to try something new; develop your skills to use technology in innovative ways to facilitate learning.

- **Know your participants.** They may be far ahead of you in their skills with technology or they may be far behind. If you plan to use learning technologies, do your best to assess their skill level before designing the workshop.

- **Be prepared for challenges.** No matter the skill level of the group, technology glitches are unavoidable. Be sure to cultivate good working relationships with technology support staff.

Key Points

- Most learning does not happen in a classroom but through multiple points of reinforcement. Learning technologies are an efficient way to augment learning.

- You can use learning technologies your organization already has if you are creative and partner with your technology team.

- Use learning technologies throughout the learning process to increase engagement, understanding, and application.

What to Do Next

- **Highlight the portions of this chapter that seem most relevant to your learning plan.** Meet with your technology team and get its input on the most applicable tools you might use.

- **Create a plan for how you will use learning technologies to reinforce your workshop.** Ensure that you select only those tools and activities that will enhance the overall learning objectives and be mindful of your organization's culture and comfort level with technology.

- **Test, test, test!** Practice using technology tools to ensure they will deliver what you hope.

- **Read the next chapter to learn ways you can improve your facilitation skills.** Many of these skills will also be useful when using learning technologies, especially collaboration tools.

Additional Resources

Bozarth, J. (2014). "Effective Social Media for Learning." In E. Biech, ed., *ASTD Handbook: The Definitive Reference for Training & Development*, 2nd edition. Alexandria, VA: ASTD Press.

Chen, J. (2012). *50 Digital Team-Building Games: Fast, Fun Meeting Openers, Group Activities and Adventures Using Social Media, Smart Phones, GPS, Tablets, and More.* Hoboken, NJ: Wiley.

Halls, J. (2012). *Rapid Video Development for Trainers: How to Create Learning Videos Fast and Affordably.* Alexandria, VA: ASTD Press.

Kapp, K. (2013). *The Gamification of Learning and Instruction Fieldbook: Ideas Into Practice.* San Francisco: Wiley.

Palloff, R.M., and K. Pratt. (2009). *Building Online Learning Communities: Effective Strategies for the Virtual Classroom.* San Francisco: Jossey-Bass.

Quinn, C. (2014). "M-Thinking: There's an App for That." In E. Biech, ed., *ASTD Handbook: The Definitive Reference for Training & Development*, 2nd edition. Alexandria, VA: ASTD Press.

Swindling, L.B., and M.V.B. Partridge. (2008). "Intellectual Property: Protect What Is Yours and Avoid Taking What Belongs to Someone Else." In E. Biech, *ASTD Handbook for Workplace Learning Professionals.* Alexandria, VA: ASTD Press.

Toth, T. (2006). *Technology for Trainers.* Alexandria, VA: ASTD Press.

Udell, C. (2012). *Learning Everywhere: How Mobile Content Strategies Are Transforming Training.* Nashville, TN: Rockbench Publishing.

Chapter 8

Delivering Your New Supervisor Workshop: Be a Great Facilitator

What's in This Chapter

- Defining the facilitator's role

- Creating an effective learning environment

- Preparing participant materials

- Using program preparation checklists

- Starting and ending on a strong note

- Managing participant behaviors

Let's get one thing clear from the get-go: Facilitating a workshop—facilitating learning—is *not* lecturing. The title of ATD's bestselling book says it all: *Telling Ain't Training* (Stolovitch and Keeps 2011). A facilitator is the person who helps learners open themselves to new learning and makes the process easier. The role requires that you avoid projecting yourself as a subject matter expert (SME) and that you prepare activities that foster learning through "hands-on" experience and interaction.

Before you can help someone else learn, you must understand the roles you will embody when you deliver training: trainer, facilitator, and learner. When a workshop begins, you are the trainer, bringing to the learning event a plan, structure, experience, and objectives. This is only possible because you have a strong, repeatable logistics process. As you ask the learners to prioritize the learning objectives, you slowly release control, inviting them to become partners in their own learning. As you move from the trainer role into the facilitator role, the objectives are the contract between the learners and the facilitator. All great facilitators also have a third role in the classroom—the role of learner. If you are open, you can learn many new things when you are in class. If you believe you must be the expert as a learning facilitator, you will not be very effective.

To be most successful as a learning facilitator, consider this checklist:

- ☐ Identify the beliefs that limit your ability to learn and, therefore, to teach.
- ☐ Learning is a gift for you and from you to others.
- ☐ Choose carefully what you call yourself and what you call your outcomes.
- ☐ Clarify your purpose to better honor your roles at a learning event.
- ☐ If you can't teach with passion, don't do it.

This last point is especially important. Not everyone is destined to be a great facilitator and teacher, but you can still have enormous impact if you are passionate about the topic, about the process, and about helping people improve their working lives. If you are serious about becoming a great facilitator, Chapter 12 provides a comprehensive assessment instrument to help you manage your personal development and increase the effectiveness of your training (see Assessment 3). You can use this instrument for self-assessment, end-of-course feedback, observer feedback, or as a professional growth tracker.

With these points firmly in mind—facilitating is not lecturing and passion can get you past many facilitator deficiencies—let's look at some other important aspects of facilitating, starting with how to create an engaging and effective learning environment.

The Learning Environment

Colors, seating, tools, environmental considerations (such as temperature, ventilation, lighting), and your attitude, dress, preparation, and passion all enhance—or detract from—an effective and positive learning environment. This section describes some ways to maximize learning through environmental factors.

Color. Research has shown that bland, neutral environments are so unlike the real world that learning achieved in these "sensory deprivation chambers" cannot be transferred to the job. Color can be a powerful way to engage the limbic part of the brain and create long-term retention. It can align the right and left brains. Ways to incorporate color include artwork, plants, and pictures that help people feel comfortable and visually stimulated. Consider printing your handouts and assessments in color. The training support materials provided in this book are designed in color but can be printed in either color or grayscale (to reduce reproduction costs).

Room Setup. Because much learning requires both individual reflection and role playing, consider seating that promotes personal thought and group sharing. One way to accomplish this is to set up groups of three to five at round or square tables, with each chair positioned so the projection screen can easily be seen. Leave plenty of room for each person so that when he or she does need to reflect, there is a feeling of privacy. Keep in mind that comfortable chairs and places to write help people relax to learn. Figure 8-1 details more room configurations that you can use to accomplish specific tasks or purposes in training.

Tools of the Trade. Lots of flipcharts (one per table is optimal) with brightly colored markers create an interactive environment. Flipcharts are about as basic and low tech as tools get, but they are also low cost and do the trick. Consider putting colorful hard candy on the tables (include sugar-free options), with bright cups of markers, pencils, and pens. Gather pads of colorful sticky notes and "fidgets" (quiet toys such as chenille stems, Koosh balls, and others) to place on the table as well. For the right level of trust to exist, your learners must feel welcome.

Your Secret Weapon. Finally, the key to establishing the optimal learning environment is *you*. You set the tone by your attitude, the way you greet people, the clothes you wear, your passion, and your interest and care for the participants. You set the stage for learning with four conditions that only you as the facilitator can create to maximize learning:

1. **Confidentiality.** Establish the expectation that anything shared during the training program will remain confidential among participants and that as the facilitator you are committed to creating a safe environment. An important step in learning is first admitting ignorance, which has some inherent risk. Adult learners may resist admitting their learning needs because they fear the repercussions of showing their weaknesses. You can alleviate these concerns by assuring participants that the sole purpose of the training is to build their skills, and that no evaluations will take place. Your workshop must be a safe place to learn and take risks.

Figure 8-1. Seating Configurations

Select a room setup that will best support the needs of your learners:

- **Rounds.** Circular tables are particularly useful for small-group work when you have 16 to 24 participants.

- **U-Shaped.** This setup features three long rectangular tables set up to form a U, with you at the open end. It is good for overall group interaction and small-group work (two to three people). This setup also helps you establish rapport with your learners.

- **Classroom.** This setup is a traditional grade school format characterized by rows of tables with all the participants facing forward toward the trainer. Avoid this setup as much as possible because you become the focal point rather than the learners, and your ability to interact with learners is extremely limited. Problems of visibility also occur when rows in the back are blocked by rows in the front.

- **Chevron.** Chevron setup features rows of tables as in the classroom setup but the tables are angled to form a V-shape. This opens up the room to allow you to interact more with the learners and accommodates a larger group of learners without sacrificing visibility. However, it shares many of the drawbacks of the classroom setup.

- **Hybrid or Fishbone.** This setup combines a U-shaped configuration with that of a chevron. It is useful when there are too many learners to form a good U and there is room enough to broaden the U to allow tables to be set up as chevrons in the center of the U. This hybrid approach allows for interaction and enables the trainer to move around.

Source: Drawn from McCain and Tobey (2004).

2. **Freedom from distractions.** Work and personal demands cannot be ignored during training, but to maximize each participant's learning, and as a courtesy to others, outside demands should be minimized:

    a. Select a training site away from the workplace to help reduce distractions.

    b. Acknowledge that participants probably feel they shouldn't be away from work; remind them that the purpose of the training is to improve their work lives.

    c. Ask that cell phones and pagers be turned off or set to silent alerts.

    d. Emphasize that because they are spending this time in training, trainees should immerse themselves in the learning experience and thereby maximize the value of their time away from work responsibilities.

3. **Personal responsibility for learning.** A facilitator can only create the *opportunity* for learning. Experiential learning requires that participants actively engage with and commit to learning—they cannot sit back and soak up information like sponges.

4. **Group participation.** Each participant brings relevant knowledge to the training program. Through discussion and sharing of information, a successful training session will tap into the knowledge of each participant. Encourage all participants to accept responsibility for helping others learn.

Program Preparation Checklist

Preparation is power when it comes to facilitating a successful workshop, and a checklist is a powerful tool for effective preparation. This checklist of activities will help you prepare your workshop:

- ☐ Write down all location and workshop details when scheduling the workshop.
- ☐ Make travel reservations early (to save money, too), if applicable.
- ☐ Send a contract to the client to confirm details, or if you are an internal facilitator, develop guidelines and a workshop structure in conjunction with appropriate supervisors and managers.
- ☐ Specify room and equipment details in writing and then confirm by telephone.
- ☐ Define goals and expectations for the workshop.
- ☐ Get a list of participants, titles, roles, and responsibilities.
- ☐ Send participants a questionnaire that requires them to confirm their goals for the workshop.
- ☐ Send the client (or the participants, if you are an internal facilitator) an agenda for the workshop, with times for breaks and meals.
- ☐ Recommend that lunch or dinner be offered in-house, with nutritious food provided.
- ☐ Make a list of materials that you will need in the room (pads of paper, pens, pencils, markers, flipcharts, and so forth). Make sure to plan for some extras.
- ☐ Design the room layout (for example, U-shaped, teaching style, auditorium set-up, or half-circle).
- ☐ Confirm whether you or your internal/external client will prepare copies of the workshop handouts. The workshop handouts should include all tools, training instruments, assessments, and worksheets. You may choose also to include copies of the presentation slides as part of the participant guide. All the supplemental materials you need to conduct the workshops in this book are available for download (see Chapter 14 for instructions).
- ☐ Find out if participants would like to receive pre-reading materials electronically before the session.
- ☐ Prepare assessments, tools, training instruments, and workshop materials at least one week before the workshop so that you have time to peruse and check them and assemble any equipment you may need (see the next two sections).

Participant Materials

Participant materials support participant learning throughout the workshop and provide continuing references after the workshop has ended. There are several kinds of participant materials. Here are some options:

Handouts

The development and "look" of your handouts are vital to help participants understand the information they convey. To compile the handouts properly, first gather all assessments, tools, training instruments, activities, and presentation slides and arrange them in the order they appear in the workshop. Then bind them together in some fashion. There are several options for compiling your material, ranging from inexpensive to deluxe. The kind of binding is your choice—materials can be stapled, spiral bound, or gathered in a ring binder—but remember that a professional look supports success. Your choice of binding will depend on your budget for the project. Because first appearances count, provide a cover with eye-catching colors and appropriate graphics.

Using the agendas in Chapters 1–3, select the presentation slides, learning activities, handouts, tools, and assessments appropriate to your workshop (see Chapter 14: Online Tools and Downloads). If you choose to print out the presentation slides for your participants, consider printing no more than three slides per handout page to keep your content simple with sufficient white space for the participants to write their own notes. Use the learning objectives for each workshop to provide clarity for the participants at the outset. Remember to number the pages, to add graphics for interest (and humor), and to include tabs for easy reference if the packet of materials has multiple sections.

Some participants like to receive the handouts before the workshop begins. You may want to email participants to determine if they would like to receive the handouts electronically.

Presentation Slides

This ATD Workshop Series book includes presentation slides to support the two-day, one-day, and half-day agendas. They have been crafted to adhere to presentation best practices. If you choose to reorder or otherwise modify the slides, keep in mind these important concepts.

When you use PowerPoint software as a teaching tool, be judicious in the number of slides that you prepare. In a scientific lecture, slides are usually a necessity for explaining formulas or results, but effective workshops rely on interaction so keep the slide information simple. Also, do not include more than five or six bullet points per slide. See more tips for effective Power-Point slides in Figure 8-2.

A message can be conveyed quickly through the use of simple graphics. For example, an illustration of two people in conversation may highlight interpersonal communication, while a photo of a boardroom-style meeting may illustrate a group engaged in negotiation. Please note that any use of the images in the presentation slides provided with this book other than as part of your presentation is strictly prohibited by law.

When you use presentation slides ask yourself: What will a slide add to my presentation? Ensure that the answer that comes back is "it will enhance the message." If slides are simply used to make the workshop look more sophisticated or technical, the process may not achieve the desired results.

It can be frustrating when a facilitator shows a slide for every page that the participants have in front of them. The dynamics of the class are likely to disconnect. If the information you are teaching is in the handouts or workbook, work from those media alone and keep the workshop personally interactive.

Workbooks and Journals

A participant journal can be included in the binder with your handouts, or it may be a separate entity. Throughout the workshop participants can assess their progress and advance their development by entering details of their personal learning in the journal. The benefit of this journal to participants is that they can separate their personal discoveries and development from the main workshop handouts and use this journal as an action plan if desired.

Videos

If you show a video in your workshop, ensure that the skills it contains are up to date and that the video is less than 20 minutes long. Provide questions that will lead to a discussion of the information viewed. Short video clips can be effective learning tools.

Toys, Noisemakers, and Other Props

Experienced facilitators understand the value of gadgets and games that advance the learning, provide a break from learning, or both.

Figure 8-2. Tips for Effective PowerPoint Slides

Presentation slides can enhance your presentation. They can also detract from it by being too cluttered, monotonous, or hard to read. Here are some tips for clear, effective slides:

Fonts

- Use sans-serif fonts such as Arial, Calibri, or Helvetica; other fonts are blurry when viewed from 20 feet or more and are more easily read on LCD screens and in video/web presentations.

- Use the same sans-serif font for most (if not all) of the presentation.

- Use a font size no smaller than 24 points. (This will also help keep the number of bullets per slide down.)

- Consider using a 32-point font—this is the easiest for web/video transmission.

- Limit yourself to one font size per slide.

Colors

- Font colors should be black or dark blue for light backgrounds and white or yellow on dark backgrounds. Think high contrast for clarity and visual impact.

- Avoid using red or green. It doesn't project well, doesn't transfer well when used in a webinar, and causes issues for people who suffer color blindness.

Text and Paragraphs

- Align text left or right, not centered.

- Avoid cluttering a slide—use a single headline and a few bullet points.

- Use no more than six words to a line; avoid long sentences.

- Use sentence case—ALL CAPS ARE DIFFICULT TO READ AND CAN FEEL LIKE YELLING.

- Avoid abbreviations and acronyms.

- Limit use of punctuation marks.

Source: Developed by Cat Russo.

Adults love to play. When their minds are open they learn quickly and effectively. Something as simple as tossing a rubber ball from person to person as questions are asked about elements studied can liven up the workshop and help people remember what they've learned.

Case studies and lively exercises accelerate learning. Bells and whistles are forms of communication; use them when you pit two teams against each other or to indicate the end of an activity.

Facilitator Equipment and Materials

When all details for the workshop have been confirmed, it is time to prepare for the actual facilitation of the workshop at the site. You may know the site well because you are providing in-house facilitation. If, however, you are traveling off site to facilitate, important elements enter the planning. Here's a checklist of things to consider:

NEW SUPERVISOR training

- [ ] Pack a data-storage device that contains your handouts and all relevant workshop materials. In the event that your printed materials do not reach the workshop location, you will have the electronic files to reprint on site.

- [ ] Pack the proper power cords, a spare battery for the laptop, and a bulb for the LCD or overhead projector in the event that these items are not available at the workshop location. This requires obtaining the make and model of all audiovisual and electronic equipment from the client or the training facility during your planning process.

- [ ] Bring an extension cord.

- [ ] Bring reference materials, books, article reprints, and ancillary content. Take advantage of all technology options, such as tablets or other readers to store reference materials. As a facilitator, you will occasionally need to refer to materials other than your own for additional information. Having the materials with you not only provides correct information about authors and articles, but it also positively reinforces participants' impressions of your knowledge, training, openness to learning, and preparedness.

- [ ] Bring flipcharts, painter's tape, and sticky notes.

- [ ] Pack toys and games for the workshop, a timer or bell, and extra marking pens.

- [ ] Bring duct tape. You may need it to tape extension cords to the floor as a safety precaution. The strength of duct tape also ensures that any flipchart pages hung on walls (with permission) will hold fast. Or, worst-case scenario, the duct tape can be used to contain unruly participants!

You can ship these items to the workshop in advance, but recognize that the shipment may not arrive in time, and that even if it does arrive on time, you may have to track it down at the venue. Also, take some time identifying backups or alternatives in case the materials, technology, and so on do not conform to plan. What are the worst-case scenarios? How could you manage such a situation? Prepare to be flexible and creative.

A Strong Start: Introduction, Icebreakers, and Openers

The start of a session is a crucial time in the workshop dynamic. How the participants respond to you, the facilitator, can set the mood for the remainder of the workshop. To get things off on the right foot, get to the training room early, at least 30 to 60 minutes before the workshop. This gives you time not only to set up the room if that has not already been done, but also to test the environment, the seating plan, the equipment, and your place in the room. Find out where the restrooms are. When participants begin to arrive (and some of them come very early), be ready to welcome them. Don't be distracted with problems or issues; be free and available to your participants.

While they are settling in, engage them with simple questions:

- How was your commute?
- Have you traveled far for this workshop?
- Was it easy to find this room?
- May I help you with anything?

When the participants have arrived and settled, introduce yourself. Write a humorous introduction, if that's your style, because this will help you be more approachable. Talk more about what you want to accomplish in the workshop than about your accomplishments. If you have a short biographical piece included in the handouts or in the workbook, it may serve as your personal introduction.

At the conclusion of your introduction, provide an activity in which participants can meet each other (often called an icebreaker). Because participants sometimes come into a training session feeling inexperienced, skeptical, reluctant, or scared, using icebreaker activities to open training enables participants to interact in a fun and nonthreatening way and to warm up the group before approaching more serious content. Don't limit the time on this too much unless you have an extremely tight schedule. The more time participants spend getting to know each other at the beginning of the workshop, the more all of you will benefit as the session proceeds.

Feedback

Feedback is the quickest, surest way for you, the facilitator, to learn if the messages and instruction are reaching the participants and if the participants are absorbing the content. It is also important for you to evaluate the participants' rate of progress and learning. Answers to the questions you ask throughout the workshop will help you identify much of the progress, but these answers come from only a few of the participants at a time. They're not a global snapshot of the entire group's comprehension and skills mastery.

When you lead a workshop, the participants walk a fine line between retention and deflection of knowledge. Continuing evaluations ensure that learning is taking root. Three levels of questions—learning comprehension, skills mastery, and skills application—help you determine where the training may not be achieving the intended results.

- Learning comprehension checks that the participants understand and grasp the skills being taught (see Figure 8-3).

- Skills mastery means that the participants are able to demonstrate their newly acquired knowledge by some activity, such as teaching a portion of a module to their fellow participants or delivering their interpretation of topic specifics to the class (see Figure 8-4).

- Skills application is the real test. You may choose to substantiate this through role plays or group case studies. When the participants have the opportunity to verbally communicate the skills learned and to reach desired results through such application, then skills application is established (see Figure 8-5).

The questions in Figures 8-3 to 8-5 are designed for written answers so you can incorporate them into the takeaway workbook you create. The questions concerning skills mastery and skills application could be used as homework if the workshop is longer than one day. Keep in mind that you will also reevaluate after each day of a multiday session.

Let's now look at other forms of in-class learning assessments: role plays, participant presentations, ball toss, and journaling.

Role Plays

Role plays are an effective tool for assessing learning comprehension. If two or more participants conduct a role play that reveals their understanding of the information, with an outcome that reflects that understanding, then it becomes a "live feed," instantaneous learning for all.

You must set up the role play carefully. It is often wise for you to be a part of the first role-play experience to show participants how it's done and to make them more comfortable with the activity. Ensure that you explain all the steps of the role play and the desired outcome. It is insightful to role-play a negative version first, followed by participant discussion; then role-play a positive aspect the second time. For example, if confrontational communication is the topic

Figure 8-3. Learning Comprehension Questions

Here are some questions that can be asked to determine each participant's level of *learning comprehension*:

- Give a brief overview of your learning in this workshop. (Begin your phrases with "I have learned. . . ." This will assist you in focusing your responses.)
- How/where will you apply this knowledge in your workplace?
- Did you acquire this knowledge through lectures/practice/discussion or a combination of all methods?
- Do you feel sufficiently confident to pass on this knowledge to your colleagues?
- Are there any areas that will require additional learning for you to feel sufficiently confident?

Figure 8-4. Skills Mastery Questions

Now let's look at some questions you can use to evaluate your trainees' *skills mastery*:

- If you were asked to teach one skill in this workshop, which skill would it be?
- What would your three key message points be for that skill?
- Describe the steps you would take to instruct each message point (for example, lecture, group discussion, PowerPoint presentation, and so forth).
- What methods would you use to ensure that your participants comprehend your instruction?
- Would feedback from your participants, both positive and negative, affect the development of your skills mastery? If yes, illustrate your response and the changes you would make.

Figure 8-5. Skills Application Questions

And finally, let's consider some questions that identify participants' *ability to apply the skills* they've learned in the workshop:

- Please describe a situation at your workplace where you could employ one specific communication skill from this workshop.
- How would you introduce this skill to your colleagues?
- How would you set goals to measure the improvement in this skill?
- Describe the input and participation you would expect from your colleagues.
- How would you exemplify mastery of the skill?

and the situation under discussion involves a line manager and his or her supervisor, first enact the role play using the verbal and body language that is causing the negative result. Discuss this as a class to identify the specific language that needs improvement. Then enact the role play again, this time using positive language.

Frequently it is helpful for a participant who has been on the receiving end of negative communication in his or her workplace to adopt the role of deliverer. Walking in the other person's shoes leads to a quicker understanding of the transaction. This positive role play should also be followed by whole-group discussion of the elements that worked. Participants can be invited to write about the process and its results to give them a real-life example to take back to the workplace.

Participant Presentations

You might ask a participant to present a module of learning to the workshop. This allows the facilitator to observe the participants from a different perspective—both as listeners and as presenters. Be ready to assist or to answer questions. For example, a participant may choose assertive communication as his or her module, and the specific issue on return to the workplace may be a request for promotion. The participant defines and delivers the steps required to ask for the promotion while the facilitator and other participants observe and evaluate the success of the approach and demonstration of confidence and assertiveness.

Ball Toss

A quick method for evaluating a class's knowledge of the material presented is to ask the participants to form a standing circle. The facilitator throws out a soft rubber ball to an individual and asks a question about the previous learning activity. When the catcher gives the right answer, he or she throws the ball to another participant who answers another question. The facilitator can step out of this circle and let the participants ask as well as answer questions to review the skills as a group. Candy for all as a reward for contributions is always enjoyed by the participants (consider keeping some sugar-free treats on hand as well).

Journaling

Keeping a journal is a quiet, introspective way for participants to get a grip on their learning. When you complete an activity, have everyone take five minutes to write a summary of the skill just learned and then ask them to share what they've written with a partner. Invite the partner to correct and improve the material if necessary or appropriate.

Questioning Skills

When participants are asking questions, they are engaged and interested. Your responses to questions will augment the learning atmosphere. The way in which you respond is extremely important. Answers that are evasive can disturb a class because they cast doubts on your credibility. Glib or curt answers are insulting. Lengthy responses break the rhythm of the class and often go off track. When dealing with questions, the value of effective communication is in hearing the question, answering the question asked, and moving on. Repeat questions so that all participants hear them. In addition, this can ensure that you have heard the question correctly.

However, don't rush to answer. Take time to let everyone absorb the information. When time is of the essence, don't be tempted to give long, complicated answers that embrace additional topics. Be courteous and clear. Check that your answer has been understood. When a question comes up that could possibly derail the session or that is beyond the scope of the topic, you can choose to record it on a "parking lot" list and then revisit it later at an assigned time. A parking lot can be as simple as a list on a flipchart. However, whenever possible, answer a question at the time it is asked. Consider answering with analogies when they are appropriate because these often help elucidate challenging concepts.

Effective questions that prompt answers are open ended:

- What have you learned so far?
- How do you feel about this concept?
- How would you handle this situation?

Any question that begins with "what" or "how" promotes a more extensive answer. Questions that begin with "why"—as in "why do you think that way?"—can promote defensiveness.

When a participant asks a confrontational or negative question, handle it with dignity and do not become aggressive. It's helpful to ask open-ended questions of the participant to try to clarify the original question. For example, ask, "What do you mean by . . . ?" or "Which part of the activity do you find challenging?" This form of open-ended questioning requires additional accountability from the participant. The reason for the confrontation may have arisen from confusion about the information or the need to hear his or her own thoughts aloud. When you are calm and patient, the altercation is more likely to be resolved. If the participant persists, you may wish to ask him or her to discuss the specifics in a private setting. More ideas for dealing with difficult participants are provided later in this chapter.

Some participants enjoy being questioned because it gives them an opportunity to show their knowledge. Others are reticent for fear of looking foolish if they don't know the answer. Because your trainees have unique styles and personalities, always have a purpose for asking questions: Will these questions test the participants' knowledge? Are these questions appropriate? Are you asking them in the style that suits the participant?

Training Room and Participant Management

When everything is in place and ready for the session, it's time to review the "soft skills" portion of your responsibilities—that is, how you conduct the workshop and interact with participants. Here are some things to consider:

- **"Respect and respond" should be a facilitator's mantra.** At all times respect the participants and respond in a timely manner.
- **Learn participants' names at the beginning of the workshop.** Focus on each participant, give a firm handshake, repeat the name in your greeting, and then mentally write the name on the person's forehead. When you have time, survey the room and write down every name without looking at nametags or name tents on the tables.

- **Manage workshop program time.** This is vital because it ensures that the goals will be met in the time allotted.

- **Read the participants' body language.** This will help you know when to pause and ask questions or to give them a stretch break.

- **Answer questions fully and effectively.** If you don't know an answer, open the question up to the participants or offer to get back to the questioner. Make a note to remind yourself to do so.

- **Add a "parking lot" to the room**—a large sheet of paper taped to one of the walls (use your own artistic prowess to draw a vehicle of some sort). When questions arise that are out of step with the current activity, ask the participant to write the question on a sticky note and put it in the parking lot. When the current activity is completed, you can address the questions parked there.

- **Control unruly participants through assertiveness of vocal tone and message.** When appropriate, invite them to help you with tasks because frequently they just need to be more physically involved. If the unruliness gets out of hand, accompany the person out of the room to discuss the situation.

- **Be sure to monitor a participant who is slower to assimilate the information.** If time permits, give that trainee some one-on-one time with you.

- **Keep your energy high.** Inject humor wherever possible. Ensure the learning is taking root.

A Word About Dealing With Difficult Participants

Much of the preparation you do before a training session will help you minimize disruptive behavior in your training session. But, sadly, you are still likely at some point to have difficult participants in your training room. Beyond preparation, you may need some specific strategies to help you manage disruptions and keep the learning on track. Figure 8-6, drawn from McCain and Tobey's *Facilitation Basics* (2004), identifies many of these behaviors and gives strategies for nipping them in the bud.

Figure 8-6. Managing Difficult Participants

THE PROBLEM	THE SOLUTION
Carrying on a Side Conversation	• Don't assume the talkers are being disrespectful; depersonalize the behavior by thinking: "Maybe they are unclear about a point in the material, or the material is not relevant to their needs." • Ask the talkers if they don't understand something. • Walk toward the talkers as you continue to make your point; this stops many conversations dead in their tracks.
Monopolizing the Discussion	• Some participants tend to take over the conversation; while the enthusiasm is great, you don't want to leave other learners out. • Tell the monopolizer that her comments are valuable and interesting, but you would like to open up the discussion to others in the group. Then call on another person by name. • Enlist the monopolizer to help you by being a gatekeeper and ensuring that no one monopolizes the conversation.
Complaining	• Don't assume someone who complains doesn't have a valid reason to do so. • Ask the rest of the group if they feel the same way. If they do, try to address the issue as appropriate. • If they don't, talk to the individual in the hallway during the break.
Challenging Your Knowledge	• Determine if this person really knows more than you do, or is just trying to act as though he does. • If he does know more, try to enlist his help in the training. • If he doesn't, ask him to provide expertise, and he will usually realize he can't and back down.
Daydreaming	• Use the person's name in an example to get her attention. • Switch to something more active. • If behavior affects more than just one person, try to find out if something work related is causing it and have a brief discussion about it.
Heckling	• Don't get upset or start volleying remarks. • Try giving the person learning-oriented attention: "John, you clearly have some background in this area; would you care to share your thoughts with the rest of the group?" • Get the attention off you by switching to a group-oriented activity.

NEW SUPERVISOR training

THE PROBLEM	THE SOLUTION
Clowning Around	• Give the person attention in a learning-oriented way by calling on her to answer a question or be a team leader. • If a joke is intended to relieve tension in the room and others seem to be experiencing it, deal with the tension head on by bringing it up. • If it is just a joke, and it's funny and appropriate, laugh!
Making an Insensitive Remark	• Remember that if the person truly didn't intend offense, you don't want to humiliate him. But you do need to ensure that the person and everyone else in the room know that you will not tolerate bigoted or otherwise inappropriate remarks. • Give the person a chance to retract what he said by asking if that is what he meant to say. If it wasn't, then move on. • If it was, you need to let the person know that the comment is not in line with the values of your organization and it can't be allowed to continue. • If the person persists, speak to him in the hallway, or as a last resort, ask him to leave.
Doing Other Work	• Talk to the person at a break to find out if the workshop is meeting her needs. • If the person is truly under too much pressure, offer to have her come to another session.
Not Talking	• If you can tell the person is engaged because he is taking notes, maintaining eye contact, or leaning forward, let him alone. • Give the person opportunities to interact at a greater comfort level by participating in small groups or in pairs.
Withdrawing	• Talk to the person at break to find out if something is going on. Deal with the issue as appropriate. • If the person feels excluded, have her act as a team leader for a turn, or ensure that all members of teams are given opportunities to participate.
Missing the Point	• If someone misses the point, be sensitive in dealing with him or her. Try to find something to agree with in his point. • Try to identify what the person is having trouble grasping and clear up the point with an analogy or an example. • Never laugh at the person or otherwise humiliate him.
Playing With Technology	• Minimize distractions by setting specific ground rules for technology use in the training room. (See Chapter 7 for creative ways to use technology to enhance training.) • Direct a training-related question to the person. • If the behavior persists, talk to the person at break to determine if there is an issue with which you can help.

Source: McCain and Tobey (2004).

When all else fails, you have a few last resorts, although you would clearly rather not get to that point. One option is to simply pull aside the individual who is disrupting the class and talk to her privately. Dick Grote (1998) suggests in "Dealing with Miscreants, Snivelers, and Adversaries" that you can often catch someone off guard by asking: "Is it personal?" The direct question will usually cause the individual to deny that it is personal. Next, you tell the person that the behavior is unacceptable and that you will speak to a supervisor or training sponsor if it continues. This often works.

However, if it does not work, you can ask to have the person removed or cancel the program and speak to the person's supervisor. Clearly, these are not options to be taken lightly, but realize that they are available when you are faced with truly recalcitrant behavior.

Follow up when you have faced a difficult situation. Take some time to reflect on the event and write down the details of what happened. If possible, get perspectives and feedback from participants who witnessed it. If outside perspectives are not an option, think about the event from the points of view of the disruptive individual and other participants and ask yourself: What went wrong? What went well? How could I manage the situation better next time?

An Unforgettable End

In Biech (2008), contributor Mel Silberman explains that

> [m]any training programs run out of steam in the end. In some cases, participants are marking time until the close is near. In other cases, facilitators are valiantly trying to cover what they haven't got to before time runs out. How unfortunate! What happens at the end needs to be "unforgettable." You want participants to remember what they've learned. You also want participants to think what they've learned has been special. (p. 315)

Silberman suggests considering four areas when preparing to end your workshop:

- How will participants review what you've taught them?
- How will participants assess what they have learned?
- What will participants do about what they have learned?
- How will participants celebrate their accomplishments?

For example, consider what you've learned in this chapter. You've developed a well-rounded picture of what it takes to create an optimal, effective learning environment, from creating an inviting and engaging space to preparing and gathering materials that will make you feel like an organizational champ. You're ready to get the training off to a productive start, to manage difficult participants and situations, and to pull it all together in a powerful way. Now jump to the end of the chapter to determine what the next steps are and take pride in the preparation that will enable you to adapt and thrive in the training room.

The Bare Minimum

- **Keep things moving.** Create an engaging, interactive environment.

- **Pay attention to the energy in the room.** Be prepared to adjust the activities as needed. Build in content that can be delivered standing or through networking activities to get participants out of their seats when needed.

- **Have fun!** If you create an upbeat tone and enjoy yourself, the participants are likely to have fun as well.

Key Points

- Facilitation is not lecturing. It's providing learning activities and support to make learning easier for the participant.

- Facilitation is not about the facilitator—it's about the learner.

- An inviting space and a safe, collaborative environment are necessary for learning to occur.

- Good facilitation starts with passion and significant attention to preparation.

- A good start sets the tone for the whole training session.

- A strong ending helps learners to remember the training and carry lessons forward into their work.

What to Do Next

- Prepare, modify, and review the training agenda. Use one of the agendas in Section I as a starting point.

- Review the program preparation checklist and work through it step by step.

- Make a list of required participant materials and facilitator equipment and begin assembling them.

- Review all learning activities included in the agenda and start practicing your delivery.

Additional Resources

Biech, E. (2006). *90 World-Class Activities by 90 World-Class Trainers*. San Francisco: John Wiley/Pfeiffer.

Biech, E. (2008). *10 Steps to Successful Training*. Alexandria, VA: ASTD Press.

Biech, E., ed. (2008). *ASTD Handbook for Workplace Learning Professionals*. Alexandria, VA: ASTD Press.

Biech, E., ed. (2014). *ASTD Handbook: The Definitive Reference for Training & Development*. Alexandria, VA: ASTD Press.

Duarte, N. (2010). *Resonate: Present Visual Stories That Transform Audiences*. Hoboken, NJ: Wiley.

Grote, D. (1998). "Dealing with Miscreants, Snivelers, and Adversaries," *Training & Development*, 52(10), October.

McCain, D.V., and D. Tobey. (2004). *Facilitation Basics*. Alexandria, VA: ASTD Press.

Stolovitch, H.D., and E.J. Keeps. (2011). *Tellling Ain't Training*, 2nd edition. Alexandria, VA: ASTD Press.

Thiagarajan, S. (2005). *Thiagi's Interactive Lectures: Power Up Your Training With Interactive Games and Exercises*. Alexandria, VA: ASTD Press.

Thiagarajan, S. (2006). *Thiagi's 100 Favorite Games*. San Francisco: John Wiley/Pfeiffer.

NEW SUPERVISOR training

Chapter 9
Evaluating Workshop Results

What's in This Chapter

- Exploring the reasons to evaluate your program
- Introducing the levels of measurement and what they measure

---

Evaluation represents the last letter of the ADDIE cycle of instructional design (analysis, design, development, implementation, and evaluation). Although evaluation is placed at the end of the model, an argument could be made for including it far earlier, as early as the design and development phase and perhaps even in the analysis phase. Why? Because the goals of the training, or the learning objectives (see Chapter 5), provide insight into what the purpose of the evaluation should be. In fact, business goals, learning goals, and evaluation of those goals are useful subjects to address with organizational leaders or the training sponsor. Trainers often begin a program without thinking about how the program fits into a strategic plan or how it supports and promotes specific business goals, but these are critical to consider before implementing the program.

However, this chapter is not about that upfront evaluation of the program design and materials; it is about evaluating the program after it has been delivered and reporting the results back to the training sponsor. This form of evaluation allows you to determine whether the program objectives were achieved and whether the learning was applied on the job and had an impact on the business. Evaluation can also serve as the basis for future program and budget discussions with training sponsors.

Levels of Measurement

No discussion of measurement would be complete without an introduction to the concepts that underpin the field of evaluation. The following is a brief primer on a very large and detailed subject that can be somewhat overwhelming. If your organization is committed to measuring beyond Level 2, take some time to read the classics of evaluation.

In 1956–57, Donald Kirkpatrick, one of the leading experts in measuring training results, identified four levels of measurement and evaluation. These four levels build successively from the simplest (Level 1) to the most complex (Level 4) and are based on information gathered at previous levels. For that reason, determining upfront at what level to evaluate a program is important. A general rule of thumb is that the more important or fundamental the training is and the greater the investment in it, the higher the level of evaluation to use. The four basic levels of evaluation are

- **Level 1—Reaction:** Measures how participants react to the workshop.
- **Level 2—Learning:** Measures whether participants have learned and understood the content of the workshop.
- **Level 3—Behavior (also referred to as application):** Measures on-the-job changes that have occurred because of the learning.
- **Level 4—Results:** Measures the impact of training on the bottom line.

These four levels correspond with the evaluation methods described below.

Level 1: Measuring Participant Reactions

One of the most common ways trainers measure participants' reactions is by administering end-of-session evaluation forms, often called "smile sheets" (for a sample, see Assessment 2: New Supervisor Training Workshop Evaluation). The main benefit of using smile sheets is that they are easy to create and administer. If you choose this method, consider the suggestions below, but first decide the purpose of evaluating. Do you want to know if the participants enjoyed the presentation? How they felt about the facilities? Or how they reacted to the content?

Here are a few suggestions for creating evaluation forms:

- Keep the form to one page.
- Make your questions brief.
- Leave adequate space for comments.

- Group types of questions into categories (for example, cluster questions about content, questions about the instructor, and questions about materials).

- Provide variety in types of questions (include multiple-choice, true-false, short-answer, and open-ended items).

- Include relevant decision makers in your questionnaire design.

- Plan how you will use and analyze the data and create a design that will facilitate your analysis.

- Use positively worded items (such as, "I listen to others," instead of "I don't listen to others").

You can find additional tips for creating smile sheets and evaluating their results in the *Infoline* "Making Smile Sheets Count" by Nancy S. Kristiansen (2004).

Although smile sheets are used frequently, they have some inherent limitations. For example, participants cannot judge the *effectiveness* of training techniques. In addition, results can be overly influenced by the personality of the facilitator or participants' feelings about having to attend training. Be cautious of relying solely on Level 1 evaluations.

Level 2: Measuring the Extent to Which Participants Have Learned

If you want to determine the extent to which participants have understood the content of your workshop, testing is an option. Comparing pre-training and post-training test results indicates the amount of knowledge gained. Or you can give a quiz that tests conceptual information 30 to 60 days after the training to see if people remember the concepts. Because most adult learners do not generally like the idea of tests, you might want to refer to these evaluations as "assessments."

Another model of testing is criterion-referenced testing (CRT), which tests the learner's performance against a given standard, such as "greets the customer and offers assistance within one minute of entering the store" or "initiates the landing gear at the proper time and altitude." Such testing can be important in determining whether a learner can carry out the task, determining the efficacy of the training materials, and providing a foundation for further levels of evaluation. Coscarelli and Shrock (2008) describe a five-step method for developing CRTs that include

1. Determining what to test (analysis)

2. Determining if the test measures what it purports to measure (validity)

3. Writing test items

4. Establishing a cut-off or mastery score

5. Showing that the test provides consistent results (reliability).

Level 3: Measuring the Results of Training Back on the Job

The next level of evaluation identifies whether the learning was actually used back on the job. It is important to recognize that application on the job is where learning begins to have real-world effects and that application is not solely up to the learner. Many elements affect transfer and application, including follow-up, manager support, and so forth. For example, consider a sales training attendee who attends training and learns a new, more efficient way to identify sales leads. However, upon returning to work, the attendee's manager does not allow the time for the attendee to practice applying those new skills in the workplace. Over time, the training is forgotten, and any value it may have had does not accrue.

Methods for collecting data regarding performance back on the job include reports by people who manage participants, reports from staff and peers, observations, quality monitors, and other quality and efficiency measures. In "The Four Levels of Evaluation," Kirkpatrick (2007) provides some guidelines for carrying out Level 3 evaluations:

- Use a control group, if practical.
- Allow time for behavior change to take place.
- Evaluate before and after the program, if possible.
- Interview learners, their immediate managers, and possibly their subordinates and anyone else who observes their work or behavior.
- Repeat the evaluation at appropriate times.

Level 4: Measuring the Organizational Impact of Training

Level 4 identifies how learning affects business measures. Consider an example related to management training. Let's say a manager attends management training and learns several new and valuable techniques to engage employees and help keep them on track. Upon return, the manager gets support in applying the new skills and behaviors. As time passes, the learning starts to have measurable results: Retention has increased, employees are demonstrably more engaged and are producing better-quality goods, and sales increase because the quality has increased. Retention, engagement, quality, and sales are all measurable business results improved as a result of the training.

Measuring such organizational impact requires working with leaders to create and implement a plan to collect the data you need. Possible methods include customer surveys, measurements of sales, studies of customer retention or turnover, employee satisfaction surveys, and other measurements of issues pertinent to the organization.

Robert Brinkerhoff, well-known author and researcher of evaluation methods, has suggested the following method to obtain information relevant to results:

- Send out questionnaires to people who have gone through training, asking: To what extent have you used your training in a way that has made a significant business impact? (This question can elicit information that will point to business benefits and ways to use other data to measure accomplishments.)
- When you get responses back, conduct interviews to get more information.

Return on Investment

Measuring return on investment (ROI)—sometimes referred to as Level 5 evaluation—is useful and can help "sell" training to leaders. ROI measures the monetary value of business benefits such as those noted in the discussion about Level 4 and compares them with the fully loaded costs of training to provide a percentage return on training investment. Hard numbers such as these can be helpful in discussions with organizational executives about conducting further training and raise the profile of training.

ROI was popularized by Jack Phillips. More in-depth information can be found in the *ASTD Handbook of Measuring and Evaluating Training* (Phillips 2010).

Reporting Results

An important and often under-considered component of both ROI and Level 4 evaluations is reporting results. Results from these types of evaluation studies have several different audiences, and it is important to take time to plan the layout of the evaluation report and the method of delivery with the audience in question. Consider the following tasks in preparing communications:

- **Purpose:** The purposes for communicating program results depend on the specific program, the setting, and unique organizational needs.
- **Audience:** For each target audience, understand the audience and find out what information is needed and why. Take into account audience bias, and then tailor the communication to each group.

- **Timing:** Lay the groundwork for communication before program implementation. Avoid delivering a message, particularly a negative message, to an audience unprepared to hear the story and unaware of the methods that generated the results.
- **Reporting format:** The type of formal evaluation report depends on how much detailed information is presented to target audiences. Brief summaries may be sufficient for some communication efforts. In other cases, particularly those programs that require significant funding, more detail may be important.

The Bare Minimum

- If formal measurement techniques are not possible, consider using the simple, interactive, informal measurement activities or a quick pulse-check during the workshop.

- Empower the participants to create an action plan to capture the new skills and ideas they plan to use. Ultimately, the success of any training event will rest on lasting positive change in participants' behavior.

Key Points

- The four basic levels of evaluation cover reaction, learning, application, and organizational impact.

- A fifth level covers return on investment.

- Reporting results is as important as measuring them. Be strategic in crafting your results document, taking into consideration purpose, audience, timing, and format.

What to Do Next

- Identify the purpose and level of evaluation based on the learning objectives and goals.

- Prepare a training evaluation form, or use the one provided in Chapter 12 (Assessment 2: New Supervisor Training Workshop Evaluation).

- If required, develop plans for follow-up evaluations to determine skills mastery, on-the-job application, and business impact.

Additional Resources

Biech, E., ed. (2014). *ASTD Handbook: The Definitive Reference for Training & Development*, 2nd edition. Alexandria, VA: ASTD Press.

Brinkerhoff, R.O. (2006). *Telling Training's Story: Evaluation Made Simple, Credible, and Effective.* San Francisco: Berrett-Koehler.

Coscarelli, W., and S. Shrock. (2008). "Level 2: Learning—Five Essential Steps for Creating Your Tests and Two Cautionary Tales." In E. Biech, ed., *ASTD Handbook for Workplace Learning Professionals.* Alexandria, VA: ASTD Press.

Kirkpatrick, D.L. (2007). "The Four Levels of Evaluation." *Infoline* No. 0701, Alexandria, VA: ASTD Press.

Kirkpatrick, D., and J.D. Kirkpatrick. (2006). *Evaluating Training Programs: The Four Levels,* 3rd edition. San Francisco: Berrett-Koehler.

Kirkpatrick, D., and J.D. Kirkpatrick. (2007). *Implementing the Four Levels: A Practical Guide for Effective Evaluation of Training Programs.* San Francisco: Berrett-Koehler.

Kristiansen, N.S. (2004). "Making Smile Sheets Count." *Infoline* No. 0402, Alexandria, VA: ASTD Press.

Phillips, P.P., ed. (2010). *ASTD Handbook of Measuring and Evaluating Training.* Alexandria, VA: ASTD Press.

SECTION III
POST-WORKSHOP LEARNING

Chapter 10
The Follow-Up Coach

What's in This Chapter

- The key role of managers in the follow-up process
- Dozens of ideas you can implement before, during, and after the workshop to help keep learning alive

---

Organizations traditionally invest more than 90 percent of their training resources in planning and delivering formal training but very little in application support. And yet study after study shows that maximizing the transfer of learning to the workplace requires immediate follow-up as well as ongoing support. Transitioning new supervisors from "I tried it" to "I'll apply it" is more effective when three conditions are in place: 1) the new supervisor is committed to the change, 2) the supervisor's manager is prepared and willing to provide the new supervisor with support, and 3) the facilitator fosters follow-up and provides tools and activities throughout the entire process.

This chapter first addresses the crucial role of the manager in effective follow-up and then gives scores of practical ideas of what you can do before, during, and after the workshop to help new supervisors continue to grow and learn. To ensure that what was learned is not "shelved" for implementation at another time but applied immediately, consider these activities to help you make follow-up contacts, promote sharing among participants, create support groups, encourage participant mentors, distribute job aids and other tools, and provide management support and coaching.

The Pivotal Role of the Supervisor's Manager

Although an organization's learning and development staff can play an important supporting role, developing employees is really up to their direct managers. Wendy Axelrod (2011), author of *Make Talent Your Business,* suggests that if managers have an attitude of "making every day a development day," participants will return from a learning event to an environment in which follow-up will be expected.

That means that one of the learning and development departments' most critical roles is to help managers learn how to develop their employees. Consider meeting with the new supervisors' managers to ask questions, garner support, and share ideas for how they can support the new supervisors once they return from the workshop.

Another simple but effective way to help managers is to connect them with exceptional resources. For example, to help managers understand their important role, you could suggest that they read the book *Help Them Grow or Watch Them Go,* which offers a rationale for development and strategies to make it happen (Kaye and Giulioni 2012).

Many more ideas to garner manager support at every stage of training are included throughout this chapter.

Before the Workshop Begins

Supporting new supervisor training—or any training for that matter—starts long before participants attend the workshop. So, in the words of Stephen Covey, "start with the end in mind" and consider these ideas before your participants ever step into your classroom:

- **Meet with managers.** Meet with the participants' managers to discuss what the manager expects from the workshop. Dana Robinson (2013) offers these examples of questions you can ask when exploring a manager's request for a training program:
  - What are the goals for your new supervisors?
  - What are the measures you use to determine a new supervisor's success?
  - What must new supervisors do more, better, or differently if your department or function is to be effective?
  - What have you observed new supervisors do that you believe needs to change?
- **Partner with stakeholders.** Work with managers and other stakeholders to help them determine how they can help their new supervisors upon returning from the workshop and to ensure that you know what skills and knowledge are imperative for the group to learn. Ask questions to determine the linkage between the workshop and the performance results the manager seeks. At the very least leave them with a list of skills that you intend to discuss in the workshop so that they can reinforce new supervisors when they

see them implementing the skills or, as the authors in *The One-Minute Manager* suggest, "catch them doing something right" (Blanchard and Johnson 2003).

- **Action plan ahead.** Several activities in the workshop help new supervisors create a plan for their future. Inform participants' managers about these plans recommending that they discuss them with the new supervisors upon returning. Consider providing workshop handouts and other content to the managers in advance to help them prepare for these vital conversations. Handouts 24-29 all contain action planning content.

- **Put support into words.** Collect messages of support from the new supervisors' managers describing how they will support transfer of the skills after the workshop. Weave these messages into your workshop.

- **Make it personal.** Before the formal learning begins, ask participants to bring to the session supervisory challenges they hope to resolve by what they learn. This commitment to learning something new helps to ensure that new supervisors follow up with themselves.

During the Workshop

Set a good example during the workshop. As a facilitator, you are in a position of influence. Participants watch what you do; so if you stress the importance of active listening or giving clear instructions, you need to model those skills as well. Try some of these ideas during the workshop that you can continue to build on after the workshop:

- **Share successes.** Tell participants how past new supervisor sessions have had a positive impact in the workplace.

- **Read messages of support from key people from the organization.** If you are an internal facilitator or working with just one organization, you might include statements from participants' line managers describing how they will support transfer after the workshop.

- **Observe the practice sessions.** Follow the rules given in *The One-Minute Manager* to deliver helpful, timely feedback to the participants (Blanchard and Johnson 2003):

  ◦ If the behavior was incorrect, correct it. Describe what you observed, point out the expected behavior, and note what needs to change. Demonstrate the correct method or steps. Then have the participant perform the task correctly.

  ◦ If the behavior was done accurately, praise it. Take advantage of someone doing a great job to reinforce the individual and to teach others.

- **Remember to use the debriefing questions.** It is only a start to learning when participants hear the "what" of your message. The most important part comes with the debriefing questions—the "so what" (so what does that mean or relate?) and the "now what" (now what are you going to do or change or implement as a result?). Debriefing reduces the gap between talking and action and forces the learning to take an implementation focus.

- **Give the last module of the workshop its due.** The "Developing Yourself" module may not seem as important as the others, when in fact it may be the most important. Once learners leave the new supervisor workshop, they need to continue to learn. Provide participants with a range of strategies for how to continue to learn the craft of being an excellent supervisor. An activity early in the workshop discusses the need for supervisors to be competent, confident, and committed. Developing themselves is the best way to help them approach the future with confidence.

- **Discover when participants will have an opportunity to implement what they are learning.** Tell them that they should watch for follow-up about this time. Prepare your support so it is ready to send "just in time." Just prior to performance reviews, for example, you could email them a tool, a checklist, or an encouragement.

At the Close of the Workshop

Many things come together at the end of your workshop. Be sure to allow enough time to discuss next steps. "What Do Great Supervisors Do Every Day" is not just a pleasant closing exercise. It should be billed as the participant's vision of what they hope to do as "great supervisors." Here are other ways to support new supervisors at the close of the workshop:

- **Create learning communities.** Ask participants to voluntarily opt into a continuing learning group. Create a wiki or a LinkedIn page where participants can ask questions, share tips, give advice, or celebrate successes. You can seed the site with questions, links to videos, or short articles.

- **Commit to practice.** Ask participants to commit to trying one new skill within the week. Perhaps they could meet with one of their employees for a developmental discussion. Ask them to publicly commit to their plans and have them text the entire group once they complete their actions.

- **Brainstorm barriers.** Plan at least an hour for participants to brainstorm a list of barriers they anticipate may prevent them from implementing some of the skills discussed in the workshop. Form small groups to tackle each of the barriers and report out ideas to overcome the barriers. Do the group a favor by compiling the ideas and sending them out by email shortly after the session.

- **Support action plans.** Several activities in the workshop help new supervisors create a plan for their future. After they complete these plans, recommend that they discuss them with their managers upon returning and ask for support in achieving their goals. Handouts 24-29 all contain action planning content.

       NEW SUPERVISOR training

- **Organize peer practice groups.** Peer practice groups can offer a great way for new supervisors to support each other as they perfect their supervisor competencies. Encourage them to organize the groups themselves. You may wish to attend their first meeting to get them started and provide resources and a suggested meeting format to ensure the peer groups are productive.

- **Encourage peer mentoring.** Near the end of the session ask participants to partner with one other person in the workshop with whom they work most closely (and ideally are in the same physical location). You can call these partnerships support buddies, accountability partners, or peer mentors, depending on your audience. Ask everyone to pick one topic from the workshop to focus on individually in the coming month. Then ask partners to sit together and interview each other about the strategies they will use to implement their chosen topic daily at work (and at home if applicable) for the next 30 days. Direct partners to schedule four weekly meetings with each other over the coming month to discuss their progress.

- **Send postcards to themselves.** At the close of the workshop, provide each participant with a postcard. Have each participant address their postcards to themselves. On the other side of the postcard, ask them to write two MVTs (most valuable tips) and two things they intend to implement from the workshop. Direct participants to select a learning accountability partner from the group and ask them to commit to contacting their partners to debrief them once they receive their postcards in the mail. Mail the postcards to arrive two to four weeks after the workshop.

After the Workshop

According to Cal Wick, a leading learning expert and researcher, most organizations still schedule facilitators in back-to-back workshops, allowing no time to follow up and support prior program participants. A few enlightened organizations have begun to recognize that making time for ongoing support results in more learning implemented back on the job. The responsibility for this ongoing support can be shared between the facilitators and the new supervisors' managers. These ideas for follow-up activities after the workshop are simple but require deliberate and sustained effort to be effective:

Facilitator Activities. As facilitator, you are uniquely placed to support your participants' continued growth and learning. After all, you've help start them on this journey; these activities will help keep them on that path:

- Follow up your session by emailing a resource to participants. It could be a topic that came up during the session, an article that you think will be pertinent and helpful, or a link to a YouTube presentation.

- Follow up your session with a quiz. Share responses with everyone and offer prizes for the best responses.

- About a week after the session, tweet participants with a simple question; for example, you could ask them to identify a new skill they have tried and then rate how successful they thought they were (suggest a 100-percent or A, B, C, D, F scale). Follow up to see what you can do to help.

- Drop a copy of *The One-Minute Manager* off to each new supervisor. Ask them to read it over the next 10 days. Then begin to text questions to the group. If you've set up a Twitter, LinkedIn, or Facebook account for your group, you can use that as well.

- Several months after the workshop, invite the participants to return for a review and celebration session where participants share their successes and review situations they needed additional knowledge or skills to complete.

- Facilitate a book club that meets over lunch once or twice each month to read and discuss supervisory, management, and leadership books. Choose a book on a relevant topic such as teamwork, engagement, or something else a team needs to learn. Assign the book as pre-reading and host the first meeting. You could also facilitate the discussion by creating an online discussion forum using a webinar or conference call format.

- Suggest that new supervisors find a mentor.

- Create short videos or podcasts about some of the topics presented in the workshop. Send the link to participants. The easiest way to do this is to interview someone, perhaps a supervisor who is well respected in your organization or one of the new supervisors who just had a breakthrough or a success.

- Reinforce the content using your workplace communication processes. Use your workplace employee newsletter, safety newsletter, intranet, or posters to reinforce key training concepts. A poster could ask "Have you reinforced your employee today?" Provide tips, funny self-assessments, and other means for your employees to apply and refine what they've learned.

- Teach managers and new supervisors how to use an After Action Report (AAR) to create a retrospective analysis on actions completed by the new supervisor.

Managers' Actions. Encourage the participants' managers to continue developing new supervisors. Share these ideas with the managers to ensure that they take on the responsibility of helping their new supervisors to keep growing:

- Familiarize managers with the skills taught in the workshop so they can correct or reinforce behaviors they observe. They can correct inaccurate behavior by describing what was observed and explaining the expected behavior. If the new supervisor models something that was learned in the workshop, the manager should praise the accurate behavior.

- Encourage managers to find other ways for new supervisors to practice supervisory or leadership skills. Leading an internal cross-functional team or a volunteer activity is good because it allows new supervisors to experiment with new skills away from their employees. Ensure that managers meet regularly with new supervisors to provide coaching along the way.

- Suggest that managers ask participants to review key concepts learned in training with others in their same position once they return to the workplace or ask them to share a skill in a team meeting.

- Encourage managers to discuss how the new supervisors' newly acquired skills and knowledge are improving as they are being used on the job. Develop a simple checklist of items that were covered in the workshop (delegation, engagement, planning, process improvement, offering feedback, and others) so that the manager knows what to look for.

- Make sure managers discuss with their new supervisors any problems they are having with transferring skills and knowledge from the workshop to the job. Managers can help remove the barriers that keep new supervisors from practicing new skills.

Additional Topics. There are hundreds of topics and nuances to topics that a supervisor needs to learn. The workshop was just a start. There is no stopping point for learning as a supervisor. Use a needs assessment to determine what topics you might want to deliver next. To help give you a head start, here are topics that the workshop touched on only briefly or not at all:

- Managing stress
- Managing up
- Neuro-Linguistic Programming (NLP) for the next level in communication
- Negotiation
- How the disciplinary action process works
- How to terminate when necessary
- Learning to learn
- Situational leadership
- The many ways supervisors need to think: creatively, critically, strategically
- Defining job roles
- Developing personnel policies
- Strategic planning
- Establishing visions and missions
- Gathering data

- Creating engaged employees
- Productive staff meetings
- Succession planning
- Building teams
- HR practices such as benefits and compensation
- Appropriate Assertiveness
- Public speaking
- Presenting to senior leadership.

And this is still only the tip of the supervisor competency iceberg. The bottom line is that there will always be a need to continue to provide knowledge and skills to new supervisors. Consider enlisting some of the new supervisors to deliver some of these topics in the future.

The Bare Minimum

Remember that most learning occurs after the workshop when new supervisors have a chance to try out the content in the real world. Stress to managers and participants how critical reinforcement is. You do this in several ways:

- Give learners the support they need to implement ideas and concepts learned in the New Supervisor Training Workshops.
- Explain to managers how critical it is for them to be a part of the new supervisors' continued growth.
- Encourage learners to continue to learn using other resources, mentoring, coaching, and other growth opportunities such as those listed here.

What to Do Next

Many ideas are presented in this chapter. Decide which ones you will do based on these guidelines:

- **Determine what is and what isn't in your control.** You can't force managers to do anything they don't want to do. And if it isn't in the budget, well, it probably isn't going to happen.
- **Maintain momentum.** Decide the best ways to get managers involved to maintain the momentum for their new supervisors.

- **Be choosy.** You can't do everything. Decide which activities provide the most bang for the buck.

- **Select something that would be a stretch for you—yes you.** Remember that you are a life-long learner too.

- **Stay connected.** Choose follow-up activities that allow you to stay in touch with your learners.

Additional Resources

Axelrod, W. (2011). *Make Talent Your Business: How Exceptional Managers Develop People While Getting Results.* San Francisco: Berrett-Koehler.

Biech, E., ed. (2008). *ASTD Handbook for Workplace Learning Professionals.* Alexandria, VA: ASTD Press.

Biech, E., ed. (2014). *ASTD Handbook: The Definitive Reference for Training & Development,* 2nd edition. Alexandria, VA: ASTD Press.

Blanchard, K., and S. Johnson. (2003). *The One-Minute Manager.* New York: William Morrow.

Kaye, B., and J. W. Giulioni. (2012). *Help Them Grow or Watch Them Go: Career Conversations Employees Want.* San Francisco: Berrett-Koehler.

Robinson, D. (2013). *Training for Impact.* San Francisco: Pfeiffer.

SECTION IV

WORKSHOP SUPPORTING DOCUMENTS AND ONLINE SUPPORT

Chapter 11
Learning Activities

What's in This Chapter

- Seventeen activities for use in the workshop sessions
- Complete step-by-step instructions for conducting the activities

---

To help you facilitate adult learning, we have designed learning activities to deploy regularly throughout the workshop. Their purpose is to challenge and engage learners by providing stimulation for different types of learners and helping them acquire new knowledge. Many of the activities in this workshop are experiential in nature—that is, learners experience something that helps them uncover the learning. Learners will go beyond the "what" did I learn and discuss the "so what" and "now what." In some cases the activities will showcase your learners and draw upon their experiences and expertise to share with the rest of the participants.

Each learning activity provides detailed information about learning objectives, materials required, timeframe, step-by-step instructions, and variations and debriefing questions, if required. Follow the instructions in each activity to prepare your workshop agenda, identify and gather materials needed, and successfully guide learners through the activity. The experiences provided by the learning activities help support the topics covered in the workshop. See Chapter 14 for information on how to download the workshop support materials.

Learning Activities Included in *New Supervisor Training*

Learning Activity 1: Embrace Your New Role

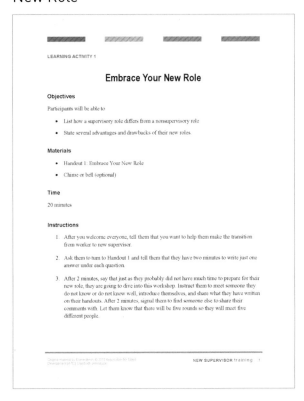

Learning Activity 1, *continued*

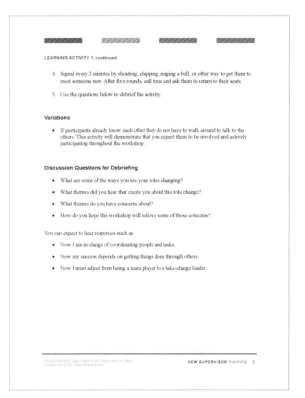

Learning Activity 2: What's Expected of You

Learning Activity 2, *continued*

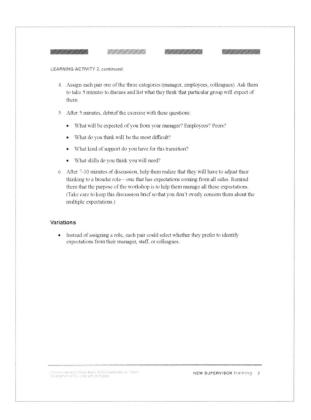

Learning Activity 3: Competence, Confidence, and Commitment

LEARNING ACTIVITY 3

Competence, Confidence, and Commitment

Objectives

Participants will be able to

- Reflect on what they hope to achieve in the short term
- List competencies they wish to attain
- Discuss what will enable them to convey confidence
- State whether they are committed to what it takes to become a supervisor.

Materials

- Handout 4: Competence, Confidence, and Commitment
- Assessment 1: Essentials of Supervision, results for reference
- Flipchart (optional)

Time

25 minutes

Instructions

1. Remind your participants that so far they've considered how their role will change and the multiple expectations that will come from various individuals. With their assessment results in hand, they can now explore their hopes for the short term. Prime the pump by asking these questions:

   - What competencies do you hope to learn in this workshop and over the next couple of weeks and months?

Original material by Elaine Biech, © 2015 Association for Talent Development (ATD). Used with permission.

Learning Activity 3, *continued*

LEARNING ACTIVITY 3, continued

- What do you need in order to demonstrate confidence—confidence not arrogance?
- How certain are you that you are committed to do, be, and believe what is necessary to be a supervisor?

2. Ask participants to turn to Handout 4 and take about 10 minutes to reflect on what has happened so far and to capture some of their thoughts on the page.

3. Give a one-minute signal and then lead them through a discussion about the three areas: competence, confidence, and commitment. Start with the easiest one: *competence*. That is what this workshop is about. Ask what they have identified as skills and knowledge they need to learn in this workshop and perhaps following it. You may wish to capture their insights on a flipchart page. Comment on those that will be covered in this session. Explain that although supervisors need to have a wide range of skills and knowledge, they should not expect to know it all now.

4. Next ask them about their *confidence* level. They may wish to explore the issue of balancing confidence so that they don't come across as arrogant or superior. They need to earn the trust and respect of their team, peers, and superiors, but they also need to do it in a way that doesn't come across as overly confident. Ask for volunteers to share what they need to do in this area. (This will be an individual need.)

5. Finally, ask whether they are ready to make the *commitment*, even with all the questions, concerns, and responsibilities that have been discussed so far.

6. Encourage several learners to share what they are thinking about this commitment.

Original material by Elaine Biech, © 2015 Association for Talent Development (ATD). Used with permission.

Learning Activity 4: Promote Communication

LEARNING ACTIVITY 4

Promote Communication

Objectives

Participants will be able to explore the important role communication plays in being an excellent supervisor.

Materials

- Handout 5: Promote Communication (one for each participant)
- 2 copies of the support material for this activity

Time

15 minutes

Instructions

1. Pick up your cell phone and read *only* Role A of the script located in the support material at the end of this activity. Treat it as if you having a phone conversation with "Mike," nodding your head, and pausing at appropriate places to give the other person time to talk.

2. When you finish reading Role A, ask participants to explain what they think might be happening in this conversation based on what they heard.

3. Ask for a volunteer to join you at the front of the room. Read the conversation again; this time ask the volunteer to read Role B of the script while you read Role A again. Pause for impact at the end.

Original material by Elaine Biech, © 2015 Association for Talent Development (ATD). Used with permission.

Learning Activity 4, *continued*

LEARNING ACTIVITY 4, continued

4. To help participants to process this activity, ask them these questions:

   - How has your perception of this conversation changed? Why?
   - Have you ever been involved in a situation where you or someone else did not have all the information?
   - Have you ever heard others make up information when they don't have all the content?

5. Now direct participants to turn to Handout 5. Ask them to examine the graph with a partner and then answer the questions on the handout.

6. Lead a debrief of the exercise by asking the questions provided below.

Discussion Questions for Debriefing

- How do you interpret the graph on this page?
- How is the survey data on feedback related to the "phone" conversation you just heard?
- Think back to before you became a supervisor. Does this data seem accurate?
- The data covers feedback on areas in which employees need to improve and how to maximize their strengths. What other situations did you feel you did not have enough communication?
- What implications does this have for you as a supervisor?

Source: Credit for this exercise is shared with Rodger Adair and adapted from E. Biech, ed., *The Book of Road-Tested Activities* (San Francisco: Pfeiffer, 2011).

Original material by Elaine Biech, © 2015 Association for Talent Development (ATD). Used with permission.

Learning Activity 4, *continued*

Promote Communication Script

Role A	Role B
1. Hey, Mike!	1. Hey bud, found the AC problem. I had to go to the attic to fix it.
2. How was it up there?	2. It was hot, but I got the AC fixed.
3. Cold?	3. Just needed to replace the filters. Now it is fine.
4. Great. For a while it got hotter than a cat with its tail on fire. Speaking of that, how is the CAT?	4. The tractor is a total loss.
5. Sorry to hear that man. I knew it was bad as soon as the fire spread through the cabin.	5. Hey, it's not all that bad. We're insured. At least you and Gramps are safe. That's all that really counts. And if Grandma had heard what happened she would end her visit with Aunt June to get back and try to fix everything herself.
6. Yeah, I miss Grandma already. As soon as those flames took out the instruments, I knew we had to get out or else!	6. Well, you did what you could. We'll be renting a new CAT to finish plowing the fields. With a new tractor we can actually bury all the seeds in one day instead of going back and covering them by hand. And Grandma won't be here to help, either.
7. Bury them? What's wrong with letting them lie around so the birds can pick at them?	7. Very funny. I'm not letting that happen this year. We have been due for a new tractor for a few years now.
8. Well, gotta go. Give my condolences to Grandpa.	8. Will do. You know how much he loved that old CAT tractor.

Original material by Elaine Biech, © 2015 Association for Talent Development (ATD). Used with permission. NEW SUPERVISOR training   3

Learning Activity 5: Share What You Know

Share What You Know

Objectives

Participants will be able to

- Recall past content related to communication and share it with other participants
- Review basic communication skills such as clear delivery, active listening, influencing others, and facilitating effective meetings.

Materials

- Handout 6: Share What You Know
- One copy of support material that accompanies this activity
- 4 flipchart stands, paper, and markers located in the four corners of the room

Time

60 minutes

Instructions

1. Say: "The late Peter Drucker often noted that more than 60 percent of all management problems are the result of faulty communication. Perhaps if he were alive today he might increase his estimate. As supervisors you need to have a solid communication foundation. All of us have had training, read books, and received practical advice about good communication. This activity will help us recall what we know to use in our supervisory roles." (Use this script until you feel comfortable with the material and then feel free to make it your own.)

Original material by Elaine Biech, © 2015 Association for Talent Development (ATD). Used with permission. NEW SUPERVISOR training   1

Learning Activity 5, *continued*

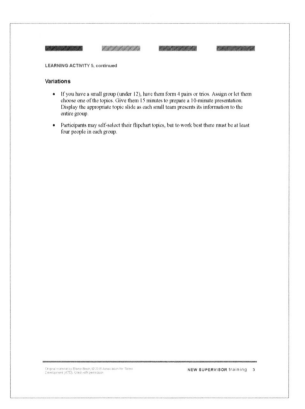

2. Break participants into four groups and assign them one of the four topics listed on Handout 6 and posted on a flipchart page in each of the four corners of the room (one topic per flipchart):

- Clear Communication Delivery
- Active Listening
- Influencing Others Based on Style
- Facilitating Effective Meetings'

3. Ask them to form their groups around the assigned flipchart, discuss their topic, and list recommendations about how to provide good communication for each on Handout 6 and on the flipchart. Tell them they have 15 minutes.

4. You probably will not need it, but if you do, a cheat sheet with a few bullet points follows these instructions to provide you with content if any of the participants have questions. This resource is for you, not the participants.

5. After 15 minutes, form new groups by asking everyone to count off by fours. Number the flipcharts 1, 2, 3, 4 and assign those with the corresponding numbers to each flipchart.

6. Ask participants to stay with their new group and move from chart to chart on a signal from you. Once they reach a chart, the participant(s) who helped to develop the content will explain it to their small group. Say that you will signal them after about 7-8 minutes at each chart and they will then move forward to the next chart as a group.

7. Encourage participants to add things to the flipcharts if they wish.

8. After 7-8 minutes, give the signal to move. The people at flipchart 1 will move to flipchart 2; those at flipchart 2 will move to flipchart 3; those at flipchart 3 will move to flipchart 4; those at flipchart 4 will move to flipchart 1.

9. Conduct a total of four rounds until everyone has reviewed all the charts.

10. Encourage participants to take photos of the flipchart pages with their smartphones for future use.

Original material by Elaine Biech, © 2015 Association for Talent Development (ATD). Used with permission. NEW SUPERVISOR training   2

Learning Activity 5, *continued*

Variations

- If you have a small group (under 12), have them form 4 pairs or trios. Assign or let them choose one of the topics. Give them 15 minutes to prepare a 10-minute presentation. Display the appropriate topic slide as each small team presents its information to the entire group.
- Participants may self-select their flipchart topics, but to work best there must be at least four people in each group.

Original material by Elaine Biech, © 2015 Association for Talent Development (ATD). Used with permission. NEW SUPERVISOR training   3

Learning Activity 5, *continued*

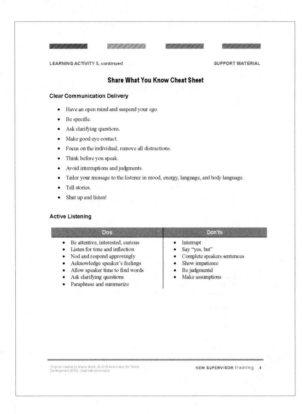

Share What You Know Cheat Sheet

Clear Communication Delivery

- Have an open mind and suspend your ego.
- Be specific.
- Ask clarifying questions.
- Make good eye contact.
- Focus on the individual; remove all distractions.
- Think before you speak.
- Avoid interruptions and judgments.
- Tailor your message to the listener in mood, energy, language, and body language.
- Tell stories.
- Shut up and listen!

Active Listening

Dos	Don'ts
• Be attentive, interested, curious	• Interrupt
• Listen for tone and inflection	• Say "yes, but"
• Nod and respond approvingly	• Complete speakers sentences
• Acknowledge speaker's feelings	• Show impatience
• Allow speaker time to find words	• Be judgmental
• Ask clarifying questions	• Make assumptions
• Paraphrase and summarize	

Learning Activity 5, *continued*

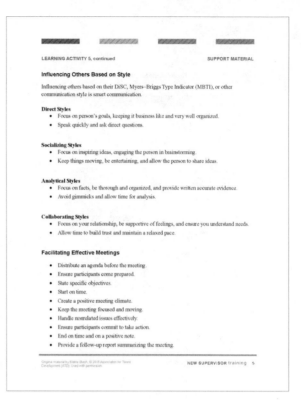

Influencing Others Based on Style

Influencing others based on their DiSC, Myers–Briggs Type Indicator (MBTI), or other communication style is smart communication.

Direct Styles
- Focus on person's goals, keeping it business like and very well organized.
- Speak quickly and ask direct questions.

Socializing Styles
- Focus on inspiring ideas, engaging the person in brainstorming.
- Keep things moving, be entertaining, and allow the person to share ideas.

Analytical Styles
- Focus on facts, be thorough and organized, and provide written accurate evidence.
- Avoid gimmicks and allow time for analysis.

Collaborating Styles
- Focus on your relationship, be supportive of feelings, and ensure you understand needs.
- Allow time to build trust and maintain a relaxed pace.

Facilitating Effective Meetings

- Distribute an agenda before the meeting.
- Ensure participants come prepared.
- State specific objectives.
- Start on time.
- Create a positive meeting climate.
- Keep the meeting focused and moving.
- Handle nonrelated issues effectively.
- Ensure participants commit to take action.
- End on time and on a positive note.
- Provide a follow-up report summarizing the meeting.

Learning Activity 6: Eggs-perience a Supervisor's Job

Eggs-perience a Supervisor's Job

Objectives

Participants will be able to

- Plan, organize, lead, and control a project using guidelines
- Define a decision-making process
- Discuss critical factors of problem solving
- Describe the delegation process
- State the importance of process improvement
- Experience change and recommend applicable actions.

Materials

- Handouts 8a-8d: Eggs-perience a Supervisor's Job
- Roll of paper towels (for accidents)
- Team supplies package (one per team):
  - 1 package of raw spaghetti
  - 6 plastic straws
  - 1 bag of regular-size marshmallows
  - 1 small package of gumdrops
  - 1 raw egg
  - 3 paper plates
  - 1 large paper bag or box to hold the team's supplies out of sight
- Flipchart paper to place at each team's building site
- Whistle or bell to announce the "change of team members" (optional)

Time

120 minutes (2 hours)

Learning Activity 6, *continued*

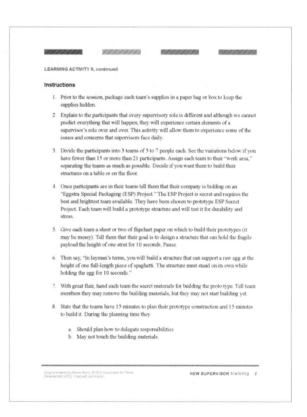

Instructions

1. Prior to the session, package each team's supplies in a paper bag or box to keep the supplies hidden.

2. Explain to the participants that every supervisory role is different and although we cannot predict everything that will happen, they will experience certain elements of a supervisor's role over and over. This activity will allow them to experience some of the issues and concerns that supervisors face daily.

3. Divide the participants into 3 teams of 5 to 7 people each. See the variations below if you have fewer than 15 or more than 21 participants. Assign each team to their "work area," separating the teams as much as possible. Decide if you want them to build their structures on a table or on the floor.

4. Once participants are in their teams tell them that their company is bidding on an "Eggstra Special Packaging (ESP) Project." The ESP Project is secret and requires the best and brightest team available. They have been chosen to prototype ESP Secret Project. Each team will build a prototype structure and will test it for durability and stress.

5. Give each team a sheet or two of flipchart paper on which to build their prototypes (it may be messy). Tell them that their goal is to design a structure that can hold the fragile payload the height of one strut for 10 seconds. Pause.

6. Then say, "In layman's terms, you will build a structure that can support a raw egg at the height of one full-length piece of spaghetti. The structure must stand on its own while holding the egg for 10 seconds."

7. With great flair, hand each team the secret materials for building the prototype. Tell team members they may remove the building materials, but they may not start building yet.

8. State that the teams have 15 minutes to plan their prototype construction and 15 minutes to build it. During the planning time they

   a. Should plan how to delegate responsibilities
   b. May not touch the building materials.

Learning Activity 6, *continued*

LEARNING ACTIVITY 6, continued

9. Announce the ending of the 15-minute planning process. Tell the teams they have 15 minutes to build the structure based on the plans they discussed. Give the signal to start the building process.

10. After 2 minutes, halt progress and say, "The company is experiencing major changes in its Innovation and Employee Engagement Program requiring each team to give up one team member for this high-level job retention taskforce. The good news is that each team will receive a replacement team member." Move one participant (*you choose*, not volunteers) from each team to a new team. Begin the timing countdown again, calling out the number of minutes left every 2 minutes.

11. Call time after the total 15 minutes. Reconvene the entire group and begin testing each structure to determine if it will hold the egg for 10 seconds. You may wish to have the entire group count off the 10 seconds while each structure holds its egg.

12. Select a couple of debriefing questions based on what is most important to your participants. Do not spend more than 10 minutes. The real learning occurs for the participants in the next steps.

13. Assign each of the teams worksheets to complete:

   - Team 1: Handout 8a, Management Functions (1 page)
   - Team 2: Handout 8b, Delegation (2 pages)
   - Team 3: Handouts 8c and 8d, Decisions, Process Improvement, and Managing Change (2 pages)

14. Tell them they have 20 minutes and they may use any resources in the room or on the Internet. After 20 minutes each team will have 15 minutes to report to the other teams. (Note: Have Teams 1 and 2 present before the break and Team 3 after. You can borrow time from the break for the activity if needed.)

15. Ask participants turn to the correct handout (8a, 8b, 8c, or 8d) as each team presents. Allow for 5 minutes of discussion after each presentation. Add any additional comments. Manage the time for the teams.

NEW SUPERVISOR training   3

Learning Activity 6, *continued*

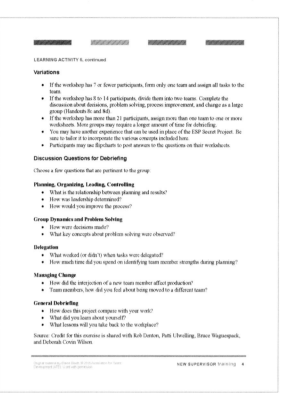

LEARNING ACTIVITY 6, continued

Variations

- If the workshop has 7 or fewer participants, form only one team and assign all tasks to the team.
- If the workshop has 8 to 14 participants, divide them into two teams. Complete the discussion about decisions, problem solving, process improvement, and change as a large group (Handouts 8c and 8d).
- If the workshop has more than 21 participants, assign more than one team to one or more worksheets. More groups may require a longer amount of time for debriefing.
- You may have another experience that can be used in place of the ESP Secret Project. Be sure to tailor it to incorporate the various concepts included here.
- Participants may use flipcharts to post answers to the questions on their worksheets.

Discussion Questions for Debriefing

Choose a few questions that are pertinent to the group:

Planning, Organizing, Leading, Controlling
- What is the relationship between planning and results?
- How was leadership determined?
- How would you improve the process?

Group Dynamics and Problem Solving
- How were decisions made?
- What key concepts about problem solving were observed?

Delegation
- What worked (or didn't) when tasks were delegated?
- How much time did you spend on identifying team member strengths during planning?

Managing Change
- How did the interjection of a new team member affect production?
- Team members, how did you feel about being moved to a different team?

General Debriefing
- How does this project compare with your work?
- What did you learn about yourself?
- What lessons will you take back to the workplace?

Source: Credit for this exercise is shared with Rob Denton, Patti Ulwelling, Bruce Waguespack, and Deborah Covin Wilson.

NEW SUPERVISOR training   4

Learning Activity 7: What's Engagement Got to Do With It?

LEARNING ACTIVITY 7

What's Engagement Got to Do With It?

Objectives

Participants will be able to list practical ways to increase engagement in their departments.

Materials

- Handout 9: What's Engagement Got to Do With It?

Time

30 minutes

Instructions

1. Ask the group what they know about engagement and take a few comments.

2. Ask them to turn to Handout 9 and follow along as you review the content on this page. Be sure to add your own content and examples. Highlight the comment at the bottom of the first page that, "all studies, all locations, and all ages agreed that the direct relationship with one's manager is the strongest of all drivers" to increase engagement. Highlight the data on the second page. Ask if this is surprising and note that it is not just "one thing" but many things.

3. Ask them to complete the Dos and Don'ts at the bottom of the handout individually. To save time, have half the room complete the Do column and half the room complete the Don't column. Tell them that they have 5 minutes to list ideas and they can jump around and fill in whatever comes to mind.

4. After 5 or so minutes, ask volunteers to share some of their insights and suggestions. Recommend that other participants add the ideas shared to their own charts.

NEW SUPERVISOR training   1

Learning Activity 7, *continued*

LEARNING ACTIVITY 7, continued

Variations

- This activity could be completed in small groups, but note that it will take more time to do so.
- If you are short of time, you could divide them into four groups. Assign each group one of these tasks:
  - Do column: start at the top and work down.
  - Don't column: start at the top and work down.
  - Do column: start at the bottom and work up.
  - Don't column: start at the bottom and work up.

NEW SUPERVISOR training   2

Learning Activity 8: Hire the Right Employee

LEARNING ACTIVITY 8

Hire the Right Employee

Objectives

Participants will be able to

- Discuss hiring elements that help locate and hire the best candidates
- Create interview questions that address what is needed for the job.

Materials

- Handout 10: Hire the Right Employee

Time

25 minutes

Instructions

1. Open by asking them to use their tablets, smartphones, or laptops to log onto any company's recruitment page (suggest a good one that you know of, such as www.qualcom.com), and click on "careers." If anyone doesn't have a device, ask people to pair up. Ask, "What do you see on the site that would attract candidates?"

2. Bring their attention to the table in the middle of Handout 10 and ask: "What could you do to improve the process currently in use?" Be prepared to add your own ideas.

3. Interview questions are the best predictors of successful hiring. Point out the examples of questions on the handout. Ask participants to use their mobile devices to search for interview questions. They should anticipate finding hundreds, maybe thousands, of questions—many in categories such as technical, culture fit, or communication skills.

4. Ask participants to share examples of creative, pertinent, or even funny questions.

5. Summarize the activity by reminding participants that hiring new employees may be one of the most important decisions they make as supervisors. Encourage them to seek out the many tools and experienced people available to help them.

Original material by Elaine Biech, © 2015 Association for Talent Development (ATD). Used with permission.   **NEW SUPERVISOR** training

Learning Activity 9: Foster Teamwork

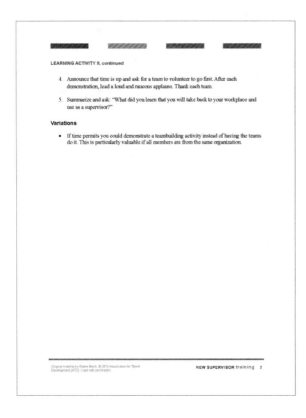

LEARNING ACTIVITY 9

Foster Teamwork

Objectives

Participants will be able to

- Review the advantages of good teamwork
- Create their own teambuilding experience and showcase it for the entire group.

Materials

- Handout 13: Foster Teamwork

Time

30 minutes

Instructions

1. If you conducted the "Eggs-perience a Supervisor's Job" activity, ask the participants to regroup into those same three teams. If you did not conduct the activity, ask participants to form three groups.

2. State that fostering teamwork is an important supervisory role. Have them turn to Handout 13, and assign one of the three questions to each of the three groups. They will have 3 minutes to develop a 3-minute response to their questions. After 3 minutes ask each team to report out in the order of the questions on the handout. Each report should be kept concise and quick—no more than 3 minutes per team. Add your own comments.

3. Tell them that now the test is whether they can demonstrate what fostering teamwork might look like. This could take the form of a communication demonstration, a flipchart picture, a teambuilding activity in which they get all participants involved, a game, a pantomime, or anything they choose. Tell them they have 10 minutes for planning a 1-2 minute demonstration.

Original material by Elaine Biech, © 2015 Association for Talent Development (ATD). Used with permission.   **NEW SUPERVISOR** training   1

Learning Activity 9, *continued*

LEARNING ACTIVITY 9, continued

4. Announce that time is up and ask for a team to volunteer to go first. After each demonstration, lead a loud and raucous applause. Thank each team.

5. Summarize and ask: "What did you learn that you will take back to your workplace and use as a supervisor?"

Variations

- If time permits you could demonstrate a teambuilding activity instead of having the teams do it. This is particularly valuable if all members are from the same organization.

Original material by Elaine Biech, © 2015 Association for Talent Development (ATD). Used with permission.   **NEW SUPERVISOR** training   2

Learning Activity 10: It Won't All Be Easy

LEARNING ACTIVITY 10

It Won't All Be Easy

Objectives

Participants will be able to

- State the three most important elements that must be in place to manage telecommuters
- Demonstrate a five-step process to resolve conflict.

Materials

- Handout 14: It Won't All Be Easy
- One copy of support material that accompanies this activity

Time

30 minutes

Instructions

1. Read the support material that accompanies this activity before you start the workshop. It gives you discussion points and background on the content discussed in the exercise.

2. Begin by explaining to that in supervising there will be many great days—and a few that will not be easy at all. Two situations with the potential to be challenging are supervising telecommuters and addressing conflict. Ask participants to turn to Handout 14.

3. Show the telecommuting slide to help introduce the three elements for successfully supervising telecommuters: having the right technology in place, utilizing good communication, and maintaining accountability. Ask participants how prepared they are in these areas and let them share a couple of their comments.

Original material by Elaine Biech, © 2015 Association for Talent Development (ATD). Used with permission.   **NEW SUPERVISOR** training   1

Learning Activity 10, *continued*

LEARNING ACTIVITY 10, continued

4. Now shift gears to a second potential supervisor challenge: dealing with conflict. Show the next slide to introduce the five steps of conflict resolution.

5. Ask participants to pair up with someone in the workshop they haven't worked with so far. Have them select a conflict situation and use the five-step process to reach a resolution. They have 10 minutes for this practice session.

6. Call time and lead a group discussion using the debriefing questions below.

Variations

- If time allows, participants could use a real example from their experience as the situation to "resolve" with their partners.

Discussion Questions for Debriefing

- What went well?
- What was difficult?
- If you could state only one thing that was most important about conflict resolution, what would it be?
- What are you taking back to your job as supervisor as a result of this activity?

NEW SUPERVISOR training   2

Learning Activity 10, *continued*

LEARNING ACTIVITY 10, continued   SUPPORT MATERIAL

Prepare for Telecommuters

More people are working remotely than ever before. Statistics show that 3-4 million professionals in the United States work from home at least once each week. (Check Global Workplace Analytics' website for the most up-to-date information as well as other resources.) Telecommuting provides outstanding benefits to both the business and the employee, but supervisors need to find effective methods for monitoring these workers. Global Workplace Analytics suggests telecommuting can be successful if you prepare in three key ways:

1. **Put the Right Technology in Place.** Use hardware such as mobile devices and web-based software programs to ensure work tasks are being managed properly. Use webinars, video-conferencing products, document-sharing tools, or other office communication services.

2. **Utilize Good Communication.** Lack of communication between team members is an issue when you don't have face-to-face interaction or the body language. Use email to communicate daily. Have a weekly conference call with the team. Host webinars to educate and train telecommuting staff on new concepts.

3. **Maintain Accountability.** Productivity can shift if you are not careful. Avoid this by developing an effective system of accountability for the team, focusing on the tasks that need to be completed and the methods for tracking progress. Web-based time clocks and project management systems can track how much time your employees are actually working. Setting the tone from the start is an important component in accountability: conduct regular check-ins beginning from day one on the job, establish scheduling deadlines, and interact with staff on a regular basis for management support and troubleshooting.

NEW SUPERVISOR training   3

Learning Activity 11: Establish a Motivating Environment

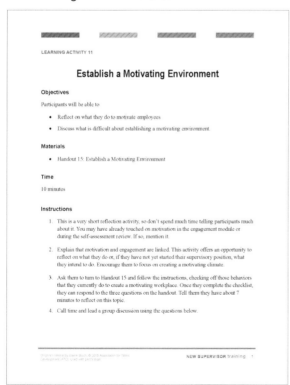

LEARNING ACTIVITY 11

Establish a Motivating Environment

Objectives

Participants will be able to

- Reflect on what they do to motivate employees
- Discuss what is difficult about establishing a motivating environment.

Materials

- Handout 15: Establish a Motivating Environment

Time

10 minutes

Instructions

1. This is a very short reflection activity, so don't spend much time telling participants much about it. You may have already touched on motivation in the engagement module or during the self-assessment review. If so, mention it.

2. Explain that motivation and engagement are linked. This activity offers an opportunity to reflect on what they do or, if they have not yet started their supervisory position, what they intend to do. Encourage them to focus on creating a motivating climate.

3. Ask them to turn to Handout 15 and follow the instructions, checking off those behaviors that they currently do to create a motivating workplace. Once they complete the checklist, they can respond to the three questions on the handout. Tell them they have about 7 minutes to reflect on this topic.

4. Call time and lead a group discussion using the questions below.

NEW SUPERVISOR training   1

Learning Activity 11, *continued*

LEARNING ACTIVITY 11, continued

Variations

- This exercise can be optional. If you are short of time, just distribute Handout 15 as a resource participants can use for planning once they return to their jobs.

Discussion Questions for Debriefing

- What do you find easiest to do when creating a motivating climate?
- How do you know what is motivating to each?
- What challenges do you face when motivating employees?
- What will you do differently when you return?

NEW SUPERVISOR training   2

Learning Activity 12: Goals, Roles, and Expectations

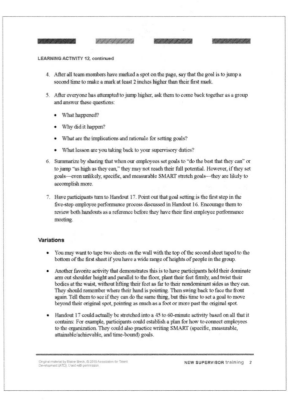

LEARNING ACTIVITY 12

Goals, Roles, and Expectations

Objectives

Participants will be able to

- Experience the value of setting a goal
- Review a resource to use back on the job.

Materials

- Handout 17: Goals, Roles, and Expectations
- One flipchart page taped high on the wall for each team (the top of the sheet should be 11 feet or more from the floor)
- Crayons or markers that do not bleed through paper, such as Mr. Sketch, ideally several different colors

Time

15 minutes

Instructions

1. Ask participants why they think goals are important and then have a few share their responses with the group.

2. Form teams of about 4-6 people and assign each team to one flipchart page that is taped to the wall. Tell each person to use a different color of marker or crayon.

3. Tell participants this is not a competition, but that they should jump as high as they can to make a mark on the paper.

Original material by Elaine Biech, © 2015 Association for Talent Development (ATD). Used with permission.   NEW SUPERVISOR training   1

Learning Activity 12, *continued*

LEARNING ACTIVITY 12, continued

4. After all team members have marked a spot on the page, say that the goal is to jump a second time to make a mark at least 2 inches higher than their first mark.

5. After everyone has attempted to jump higher, ask them to come back together as a group and answer these questions:

- What happened?
- Why did it happen?
- What are the implications and rationale for setting goals?
- What lesson are you taking back to your supervisory duties?

6. Summarize by sharing that when our employees set goals to "do the best that they can" or to jump "as high as they can," they may not reach their full potential. However, if they set goals—even unlikely, specific, and measurable SMART stretch goals—they are likely to accomplish more.

7. Have participants turn to Handout 17. Point out that goal setting is the first step in the five-step employee performance process discussed in Handout 16. Encourage them to review both handouts as a reference before they have their first employee performance meeting.

Variations

- You may want to tape two sheets on the wall with the top of the second sheet taped to the bottom of the first sheet if you have a wide range of heights of people in the group.

- Another favorite activity that demonstrates this is to have participants hold their dominate arm out shoulder height and parallel to the floor, plant their feet firmly, and twist their bodies at the waist, without lifting their feet as far to their nondominant sides as they can. They should remember where their hand is pointing. Then swing back to face the front again. Tell them to see if they can do the same thing, but this time to set a goal to move beyond their original spot, pointing as much as a foot or more past the original spot.

- Handout 17 could actually be stretched into a 45 to 60-minute activity based on all that it contains. For example, participants could establish a plan for how to connect employees to the organization. They could also practice writing SMART (specific, measurable, attainable/achievable, and time-bound) goals.

Original material by Elaine Biech, © 2015 Association for Talent Development (ATD). Used with permission.   NEW SUPERVISOR training   2

Learning Activity 13: Continuous Feedback

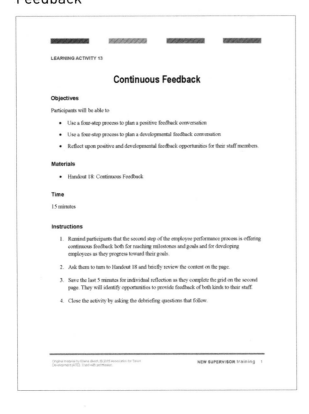

LEARNING ACTIVITY 13

Continuous Feedback

Objectives

Participants will be able to

- Use a four-step process to plan a positive feedback conversation
- Use a four-step process to plan a developmental feedback conversation
- Reflect upon positive and developmental feedback opportunities for their staff members.

Materials

- Handout 18: Continuous Feedback

Time

15 minutes

Instructions

1. Remind participants that the second step of the employee performance process is offering continuous feedback both for reaching milestones and goals and for developing employees as they progress toward their goals.

2. Ask them to turn to Handout 18 and briefly review the content on the page.

3. Save the last 5 minutes for individual reflection as they complete the grid on the second page. They will identify opportunities to provide feedback of both kinds to their staff.

4. Close the activity by asking the debriefing questions that follow.

Original material by Elaine Biech, © 2015 Association for Talent Development (ATD). Used with permission.   NEW SUPERVISOR training   1

Learning Activity 13, *continued*

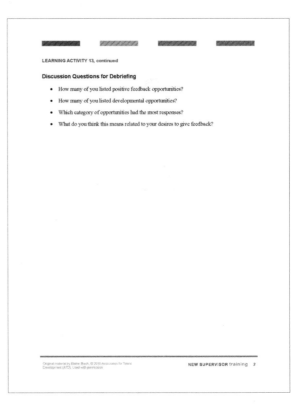

LEARNING ACTIVITY 13, continued

Discussion Questions for Debriefing

- How many of you listed positive feedback opportunities?
- How many of you listed developmental opportunities?
- Which category of opportunities had the most responses?
- What do you think this means related to your desires to give feedback?

Original material by Elaine Biech, © 2015 Association for Talent Development (ATD). Used with permission.   NEW SUPERVISOR training   2

Learning Activity 14: Feedback Practice

LEARNING ACTIVITY 14

Feedback Practice

Objectives

Participants will be able to practice and receive feedback on their own feedback skills.

Materials

- Handout 20: Feedback Practice

Time

30 minutes

Instructions

1. Ask participants to turn to Handout 20. Explain that this is a meta feedback activity where they will receive feedback on their feedback skills. Review the instructions on the handout and ask them to select one of the scenarios or to use one of their own. The goal is to practice giving feedback. Instruct them to take 3 minutes to write notes on the page in preparation for their feedback practice.

2. Ask them to partner with someone from whom they want to receive feedback. Partners should find a place to sit so that their practice will be least disruptive to others.

3. Give a signal half way through the time period and direct them to switch to the second partner's practice.

4. Debrief the activity with the entire group by asking this question: What's the most important lesson you are taking from this activity?

Variations

- If you have time you could take this to the next level of feedback. Each partner could give feedback to the person giving feedback!

Original material by Elaine Biech, © 2015 Association for Talent Development (ATD). Used with permission. **NEW SUPERVISOR** training

Learning Activity 15: Rewards and Recognition

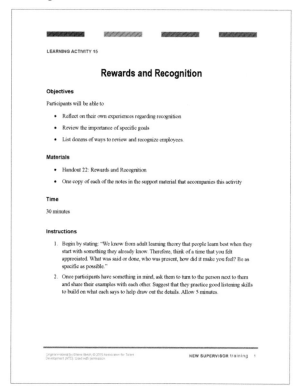

LEARNING ACTIVITY 15

Rewards and Recognition

Objectives

Participants will be able to

- Reflect on their own experiences regarding recognition
- Review the importance of specific goals
- List dozens of ways to review and recognize employees.

Materials

- Handout 22: Rewards and Recognition
- One copy of each of the notes in the support material that accompanies this activity

Time

30 minutes

Instructions

1. Begin by stating: "We know from adult learning theory that people learn best when they start with something they already know. Therefore, think of a time that you felt appreciated. What was said or done, who was present, how did it make you feel? Be as specific as possible."

2. Once participants have something in mind, ask them to turn to the person next to them and share their examples with each other. Suggest that they practice good listening skills to build on what each says to help draw out the details. Allow 5 minutes.

Original material by Elaine Biech, © 2015 Association for Talent Development (ATD). Used with permission. **NEW SUPERVISOR** training 1

Learning Activity 15, *continued*

LEARNING ACTIVITY 15, continued

3. Ask for volunteers to share a brief description of their examples. After three people have shared, say: "We already have learned two things: First, no one mentioned money. I've done this activity done hundreds of times and no one mentions money. Second, few of the items that were shared even require money. We can conclude that feeling valued and appreciated is more a function of how you are treated by colleagues you hold in high regard than what it cost.

4. Ask them to turn to Handout 22 and provide a very brief overview of what they will find there—a good resource they can use back on the job. Suggest that they dog-ear the page or mark it with a sticky note.

5. Now you are going to give them a chance to practice. Divide the group into three teams. (If you completed Learning Activity 6: Eggs-perience a Supervisor's Job, place participants into the same teams. If not, any three equal-sized groups will work.)

6. Tell them it is a contest and you would like them to move far enough apart so that the teams cannot overhear each other's task or ideas. Once the teams are settled say, "Each team has an assignment on a slip of paper. After I distribute all three sheets, you may look at them and share them within your team, but do not read the instructions out loud. Talk among yourselves, but don't let the other teams hear your task or your ideas. You will have 8 minutes to complete your tasks. You may begin now."

7. At the end of the 8 minutes, call time. Ask each team to count the number of ideas they were able to list. Teams 1 and 2 usually have about the same number on their lists. Team 3 typically blows away the competition.

8. Beginning with Team 1, ask teams to read their assignment out loud and how many ideas they listed.

9. Summarize with a discussion around these questions:

   - How were the three tasks different?
   - How do you think the different wording of the tasks affected the results?
   - What were you measuring yourselves against to determine success?
   - What can you surmise based on the results?
   - What advice can you take away from this exercise?

Original material by Elaine Biech, © 2015 Association for Talent Development (ATD). Used with permission. **NEW SUPERVISOR** training 2

Learning Activity 15, *continued*

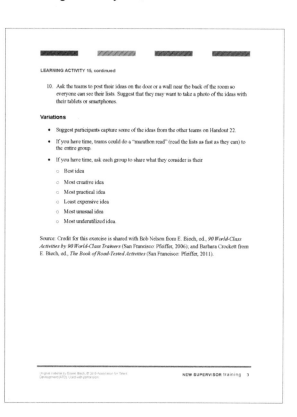

LEARNING ACTIVITY 15, continued

10. Ask the teams to post their ideas on the door or a wall near the back of the room so everyone can see their lists. Suggest that they may want to take a photo of the ideas with their tablets or smartphones.

Variations

- Suggest participants capture some of the ideas from the other teams on Handout 22.
- If you have time, teams could do a "marathon read" (read the lists as fast as they can) to the entire group.
- If you have time, ask each group to share what they consider is their
  - Best idea
  - Most creative idea
  - Most practical idea
  - Least expensive idea
  - Most unusual idea
  - Most underutilized idea.

Source: Credit for this exercise is shared with Bob Nelson from E. Biech, ed., *90 World-Class Activities by 90 World-Class Trainers* (San Francisco: Pfeiffer, 2006); and Barbara Crockett from E. Biech, ed., *The Book of Road-Tested Activities* (San Francisco: Pfeiffer, 2011).

Original material by Elaine Biech, © 2015 Association for Talent Development (ATD). Used with permission. **NEW SUPERVISOR** training 3

Learning Activity 15, *continued*

Team 1 Note

Do not let the other teams hear your ideas or your task.

List as many ideas for rewarding and recognizing your employees as you can on this sheet of paper.

Original material by Elaine Biech, © 2015 Association for Talent Development (ATD). Used with permission.

Learning Activity 15, *continued*

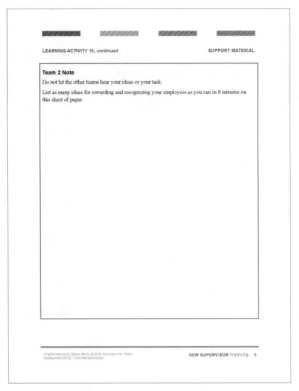

Team 2 Note

Do not let the other teams hear your ideas or your task.

List as many ideas for rewarding and recognizing your employees as you can in 8 minutes on this sheet of paper.

Original material by Elaine Biech, © 2015 Association for Talent Development (ATD). Used with permission.

Learning Activity 15, *continued*

Team 3 Note

Do not let the other teams hear your ideas or your task.

List 50 ideas for rewarding and recognizing your employees in 8 minutes on this sheet of paper.

Original material by Elaine Biech, © 2015 Association for Talent Development (ATD). Used with permission.

Learning Activity 16: How Do You Model Excellence?

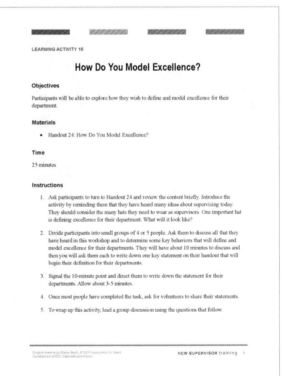

How Do You Model Excellence?

Objectives

Participants will be able to explore how they wish to define and model excellence for their department.

Materials

- Handout 24: How Do You Model Excellence?

Time

25 minutes

Instructions

1. Ask participants to turn to Handout 24 and review the content briefly. Introduce the activity by reminding them that they have heard many ideas about supervising today. They should consider the many hats they need to wear as supervisors. One important hat is defining excellence for their department. What will it look like?

2. Divide participants into small groups of 4 or 5 people. Ask them to discuss all that they have heard in this workshop and to determine some key behaviors that will define and model excellence for their departments. They will have about 10 minutes to discuss and then you will ask them each to write down one key statement on their handout that will begin their definition for their departments.

3. Signal the 10-minute point and direct them to write down the statement for their departments. Allow about 3-5 minutes.

4. Once most people have completed the task, ask for volunteers to share their statements.

5. To wrap up this activity, lead a group discussion using the questions that follow:

Original material by Elaine Biech, © 2015 Association for Talent Development (ATD). Used with permission.

Learning Activity 16, *continued*

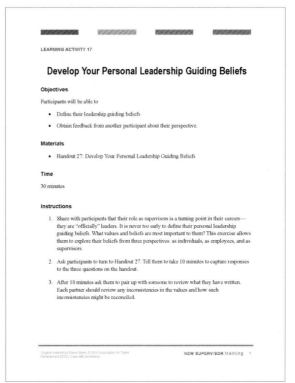

LEARNING ACTIVITY 16, continued

Discussion Questions for Debriefing

- How will you implement this once you return to work?
- What is one practical thing you will do that models this for your department? How will you "walk the talk"?
- How will you involve your staff?

Learning Activity 17: Develop Your Personal Leadership Guiding Beliefs

LEARNING ACTIVITY 17

Develop Your Personal Leadership Guiding Beliefs

Objectives

Participants will be able to

- Define their leadership guiding beliefs
- Obtain feedback from another participant about their perspective.

Materials

- Handout 27: Develop Your Personal Leadership Guiding Beliefs

Time

30 minutes

Instructions

1. Share with participants that their role as supervisors is a turning point in their careers—they are "officially" leaders. It is never too early to define their personal leadership guiding beliefs. What values and beliefs are most important to them? This exercise allows them to explore their beliefs from three perspectives: as individuals, as employees, and as supervisors.

2. Ask participants to turn to Handout 27. Tell them to take 10 minutes to capture responses to the three questions on the handout.

3. After 10 minutes ask them to pair up with someone to review what they have written. Each partner should review any inconsistencies in the values and how such inconsistencies might be reconciled.

Learning Activity 17, *continued*

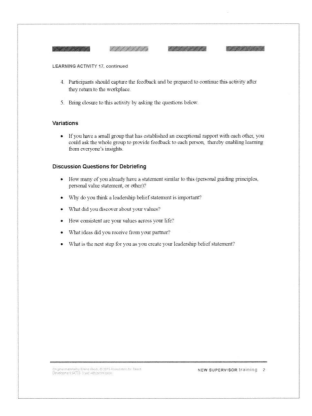

LEARNING ACTIVITY 17, continued

4. Participants should capture the feedback and be prepared to continue this activity after they return to the workplace.

5. Bring closure to this activity by asking the questions below.

Variations

- If you have a small group that has established an exceptional rapport with each other, you could ask the whole group to provide feedback to each person, thereby enabling learning from everyone's insights.

Discussion Questions for Debriefing

- How many of you already have a statement similar to this (personal guiding principles, personal value statement, or other)?
- Why do you think a leadership belief statement is important?
- What did you discover about your values?
- How consistent are your values across your life?
- What ideas did you receive from your partner?
- What is the next step for you as you create your leadership belief statement?

Chapter 12
Assessments

What's in This Chapter

- Three assessments to use in the workshop sessions or as professional development

- Instructions on how and when to use the assessments

Assessments and evaluations are critical to a workshop—before it begins, as it goes on, and when it concludes. To prepare an effective workshop for participants, you have to assess their needs and those of their organization. Although a formal needs assessment is outside the scope of this book, the self-assessment in this chapter, Assessment 1: Essentials of Supervision, can help you identify what participants' current knowledge of the topic may be. This information can help you make course adjustments to fit the needs of the learners and the organization during the workshop.

Using assessments during the workshop helps participants identify areas of strength and weakness, enabling them to capitalize on their strengths and improve their weaknesses to become more effective in the workplace. You may have participants refer back to their self-assessment during the workshop to check in on participants' learning so that all of you can make needed adjustments as you go.

Assessments of the workshop and the facilitator are vital for both the hiring organization and you as the facilitator. To learn if you met the goals and expectations, you will want direct responses from participants. Although negative comments can be tough to read, ultimately they allow you to continually learn and improve your skills as a learning facilitator. Assessment 2: New Supervisor Training Workshop Evaluation provides a form you can use as an workshop evaluation.

In addition, Assessment 3: Facilitator Competencies provides an instrument to help you manage your professional development and increase the effectiveness of your training sessions. You can use this tool in a number of ways: self-assessment, end-of-course feedback, observer feedback, or as a gauge for tracking professional growth with repeated ratings.

The assessments in this chapter provide instructions on how to complete the assessment and when to use it in the course of the workshop, as well as an explanation of the assessment's purpose.

Assessments Included in *New Supervisor Training*

Assessment 1: Essentials of Supervision

Assessment 2: New Supervisor Training Workshop Evaluation

Assessment 3: Facilitator Competencies

Assessment 1: Essentials of Supervision

Assessment 1, *continued*

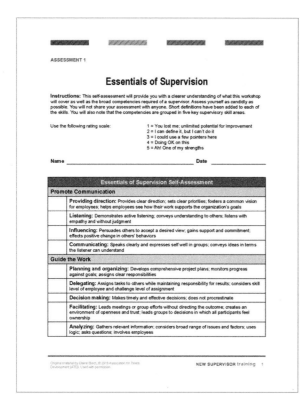

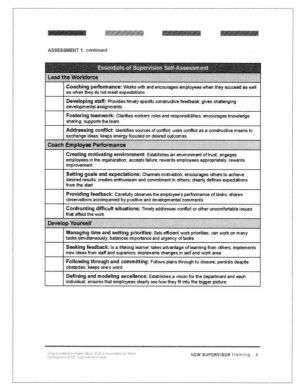

Assessment 2: New Supervisor Training Workshop Evaluation

Assessment 3: Facilitator Competencies

Assessment 3, *continued*

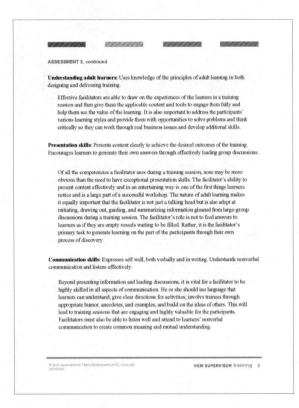

Understanding adult learners: Uses knowledge of the principles of adult learning in both designing and delivering training.

Effective facilitators are able to draw on the experiences of the learners in a training session and then give them the applicable content and tools to engage them fully and help them see the value of the learning. It is also important to address the participants' various learning styles and provide them with opportunities to solve problems and think critically so they can work through real business issues and develop additional skills.

Presentation skills: Presents content clearly to achieve the desired outcomes of the training. Encourages learners to generate their own answers through effectively leading group discussions.

Of all the competencies a facilitator uses during a training session, none may be more obvious than the need to have exceptional presentation skills. The facilitator's ability to present content effectively and in an entertaining way is one of the first things learners notice and is a large part of a successful workshop. The nature of adult learning makes it equally important that the facilitator is not just a talking head but is also adept at initiating, drawing out, guiding, and summarizing information gleaned from large-group discussions during a training session. The facilitator's role is not to feed answers to learners as if they are empty vessels waiting to be filled. Rather, it is the facilitator's primary task to generate learning on the part of the participants through their own process of discovery.

Communication skills: Expresses self well, both verbally and in writing. Understands nonverbal communication and listens effectively.

Beyond presenting information and leading discussions, it is vital for a facilitator to be highly skilled in all aspects of communication. He or she should use language that learners can understand; give clear directions for activities; involve trainees through appropriate humor, anecdotes, and examples; and build on the ideas of others. This will lead to training sessions that are engaging and highly valuable for the participants. Facilitators must also be able to listen well and attend to learners' nonverbal communication to create common meaning and mutual understanding.

Assessment 3, *continued*

Emotional intelligence: Respects learners' viewpoints, knowledge, and experience. Recognizes and responds appropriately to others' feelings, attitudes, and concerns.

Because learners may have many different backgrounds, experience levels, and opinions in the same training sessions, facilitators must be able to handle a variety of situations and conversations well, and be sensitive to others' emotions. They must pay close attention to the dynamics in the room, be flexible enough to make immediate changes to activities during training to meet the needs of learners, and create an open and trusting learning environment. Attendees should feel comfortable expressing their opinions, asking questions, and participating in activities without fear of repercussion or disapproval. Monitoring learners' emotions during a training session also helps the facilitator gauge when it may be time to change gears if conflict arises, if discussion needs to be refocused on desired outcomes, or if there is a need to delve deeper into a topic to encourage further learning.

Training methods: Varies instructional approaches to address different learning styles and hold learners' interest.

All learners have preferred learning styles, and one of the keys to effective training facilitation is to use a variety of methods to address them. Some people are more visual ("see it") learners, and others are more auditory ("hear it") or kinesthetic ("do it") learners. An effective facilitator must be familiar with a variety of training methods to tap into each participant's style(s) and maintain interest during the training session. These methods may include such activities as small group activities, individual exercises, case studies, role plays, simulations, and games.

Subject matter expertise: Possesses deep knowledge of training content and applicable experience to draw upon.

Facilitators must have solid background knowledge of the training topic at hand and be able to share related experience to help learners connect theory to real-world scenarios. Anecdotes and other examples to illustrate how the training content relates to participants' circumstances and work can enhance the learning experience and encourage learners to apply the information and also to use the tools they have been given. It is also crucial that facilitators know their topics inside and out, so they can answer the trainees' questions and guide them toward problem-solving and skill development.

Assessment 3, *continued*

Questioning skills: Asks questions in a way that stimulates learners' understanding and curiosity. Encourages critical thinking.

An effective questioning technique works well to assess learners' understanding of training content. It also provides opportunities for them to analyze information and think critically. When learners ask questions, the facilitator is able to see where there may be confusion or a need to review concepts for better understanding. Similarly, when a facilitator asks thought-provoking questions in a way that invites participation, learners can brainstorm solutions to problems or think about situations to help them apply the training content to the issues they deal with on a regular basis.

Eliciting behavior change: Influences others effectively both individually and within groups. Gains support and commitment from others to achieve common goals and desired outcomes.

This competency is important in two ways. First, facilitators must be able to persuade trainees to consider points of view that will lead to desired changes in behavior. A facilitator is often called upon to sell an organization's culture or policies, or to gain learners' participation to achieve the desired results of the training. To do this, a facilitator must be able to show that although he or she respects the trainees' views, the trainees must understand and accept the organization's realities and practices.

Second, an effective facilitator must know how to form small groups and work well with them to influence groups to accomplish tasks, work through problems, and fulfill the needs of the group members. Drawing out the creative energy of groups through brainstorming or other activities, as well as helping group members blend their unique knowledge and skills to achieve a common goal, will lead to greater commitment on behalf of the learners to improve their behavior and apply the training content.

Feedback: Gives and receives constructive, specific, and timely feedback, and communicates observations clearly and accurately.

It is essential for facilitators to provide learners with helpful feedback, whether formally through an assessment or informally through conversation. Use specific examples to communicate a learner's strengths and weaknesses; this will help the learner understand the information and may also increase the learner's self-reflection. It can also serve as the basis for a coaching relationship for individual training and clarify what the learner should focus on for his or her growth and development. The facilitator should also be

Assessment 3, *continued*

familiar with a variety of tools to gather feedback from training participants to improve the learning experience and the facilitator's own self-reflection and growth.

Motivation: Encourages learners to participate and achieve desired results. Generates enthusiasm and commitment from others.

It is the training facilitator's responsibility to inspire others to achieve the desired outcomes of a training session and to focus on their goals. Although it is generally believed that motivation comes from within, a skilled facilitator can unleash energy and enthusiasm by creating a vision that inspires the learners. Facilitators can provide meaningful learning activities and infuse fun into the training experience, and they must effectively channel trainees' motivation into a commitment to achieving results.

Organizational skills: Works in an orderly and logical way to accomplish tasks. Ensures that work is correct and complete. Presents ideas logically and sequentially for learners to understand.

The importance of this competency for facilitators is twofold. First, the facilitator must have good work habits and pay attention to detail. With any training event, many factors are necessary to ensure a successful experience. Work must be done thoroughly and accurately. A well-organized training facilitator typically creates well-organized, professional training. Second, it is important for facilitators to present ideas in a logical, sequential order that allows learners to absorb new content easily and also to be able to retrieve it quickly. This also increases the probability that the learners will actually use the content. The more organized the facilitator, the better.

Time management: Plans and uses time effectively. Balances important and urgent tasks and can work on multiple tasks simultaneously.

Facilitators do many things in addition to conducting training sessions. They must also budget their time effectively to address other priorities in their work: prepare for the training, keep accurate records, analyze assessment data, design new content or activities, and report to the client organization. The most competent facilitators are able to multitask and keep the goals of the client and client organization in view as much as possible. Good time management helps a facilitator keep track of all there is to do during any given day.

Assessment 3, *continued*

Assessment 3, *continued*

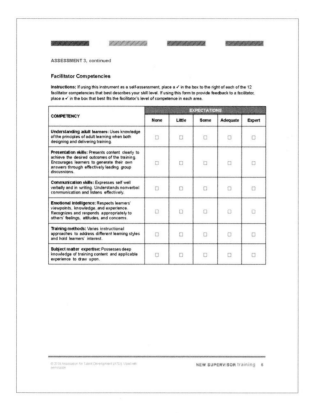

ASSESSMENT 3, continued

Facilitator Competencies

Instructions: If using this instrument as a self-assessment, place a ✓ in the box to the right of each of the 12 facilitator competencies that best describes your skill level. If using this form to provide feedback to a facilitator, place a ✓ in the box best fits the facilitator's level of competence in each area.

COMPETENCY	EXPECTATIONS				
	None	Little	Some	Adequate	Expert
Understanding adult learners: Uses knowledge of the principles of adult learning when both designing and delivering training.	☐	☐	☐	☐	☐
Presentation skills: Presents content clearly to achieve the desired outcomes of the training. Encourages learners to generate their own answers through effectively leading group discussions.	☐	☐	☐	☐	☐
Communication skills: Expresses self well verbally and in writing. Understands nonverbal communication and listens effectively.	☐	☐	☐	☐	☐
Emotional intelligence: Respects learners' viewpoints, knowledge, and experience. Recognizes and responds appropriately to others' feelings, attitudes, and concerns.	☐	☐	☐	☐	☐
Training methods: Varies instructional approaches to address different learning styles and hold learners' interest.	☐	☐	☐	☐	☐
Subject matter expertise: Possesses deep knowledge of training content and applicable experience to draw upon.	☐	☐	☐	☐	☐

ASSESSMENT 3, continued

COMPETENCY	EXPECTATIONS				
	None	Little	Some	Adequate	Expert
Questioning skills: Asks questions in a way that stimulates learners' understanding and curiosity. Encourages critical thinking.	☐	☐	☐	☐	☐
Eliciting behavior change: Influences others effectively, both individually and within groups. Gains support and commitment from others to achieve common goals and desired outcomes.	☐	☐	☐	☐	☐
Feedback: Gives and receives constructive, specific, and timely feedback and communicates observations clearly and accurately.	☐	☐	☐	☐	☐
Motivation: Encourages learners to participate and achieve desired results. Generates enthusiasm and commitment from others.	☐	☐	☐	☐	☐
Organizational skills: Works in an orderly and logical way to accomplish tasks. Ensures work is correct and complete. Presents ideas logically and sequentially for learners to understand.	☐	☐	☐	☐	☐
Time management: Plans and uses time effectively. Balances important and urgent tasks and can work on multiple tasks simultaneously.	☐	☐	☐	☐	☐

Chapter 13
Handouts

What's in This Chapter

- Thirty handouts in thumbnail format for reference
- Refer to Chapter 14 for instructions to download full-size handouts

---

Handouts comprise the various materials you will provide to the learners throughout the course of the workshop. In some cases, the handouts will simply provide instructions for worksheets to complete, places to take notes, and so forth. In other cases, they will provide important and practical materials for use in and out of the training room, such as reference materials, tip sheets, samples of completed forms, flowcharts, and other useful content.

The workshop agendas in Chapters 1-3 and the learning activities in Chapter 11 provide instructions for how and when to use the handouts within the context of the workshop. See Chapter 14 for complete instructions on how to download the workshop support materials.

Handouts Included in *New Supervisor Training*
Workshop Opening: Embrace Your Role

Handout 1: Embrace Your New Role

Handout 2: New Supervisor Skills Training Objectives

Handout 3: What's Expected of You

Handout 4: Competence, Confidence, and Commitment

Module I: Promote Communication

Handout 5: Promote Communication

Handout 6: Share What You Know

Module II: Guide the Work

Handout 7: Guide the Work—With a 21st-Century Caveat

Handout 8a: Eggs-perience a Supervisor's Job: Management Functions

Handout 8b: Eggs-perience a Supervisor's Job: Delegation

Handout 8c: Eggs-perience a Supervisor's Job: Making Decisions and Solving Problems

Handout 8d: Eggs-perience a Supervisor's Job: Process Improvement and Managing Change

Handout 9: What's Engagement Got to Do With It?

Module III: Lead the Workforce

Handout 10: Hire the Right Employee

Handout 11: Orient New Employees

Handout 12: Develop Individuals

Handout 13: Foster Teamwork

Handout 14: It Won't All Be Easy

Module IV: Coach Employee Performance

Handout 15: Establish a Motivating Environment

Handout 16: Five-Step Employee Performance Process

Handout 17: Goals, Roles, and Expectations

Handout 18: Continuous Feedback

Handout 19: Conduct Effective Performance Reviews

Handout 20: Feedback Practice

Handout 21: Negative Feedback Isn't Fun

Handout 22: Rewards, Recognition, and Retention

Handout 23: Retain Your Best

Module V: Develop Yourself

Handout 24: How Do You Model Excellence?

Handout 25: Manage Your Time

Handout 26: Get Better All the Time: Your Professional Development

Handout 27: Develop Your Personal Leadership Guiding Beliefs

Handout 28: Action Planning: My Next Steps

Handout 29: What Do Great Supervisors Do Every Day?

Handout 30: Reading List for Your Continued Development

Handout 1: Embrace Your New Role

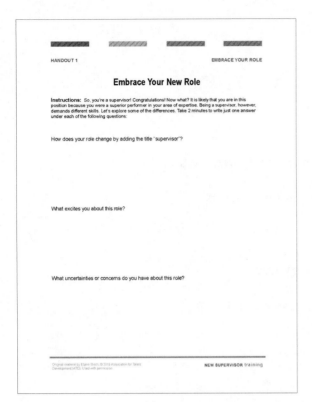

Handout 2: New Supervisor Skills Training Objectives

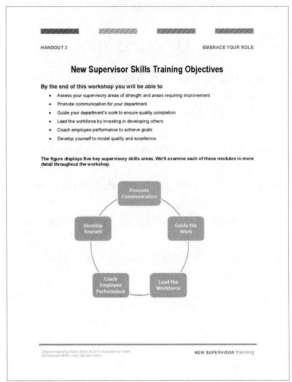

Handout 3: What's Expected of You

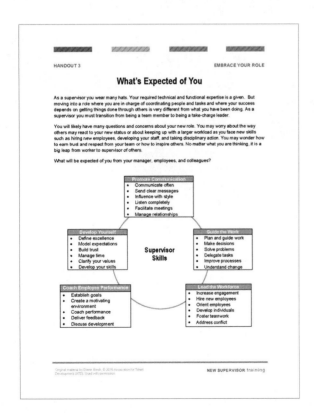

Handout 4: Competence, Confidence, and Commitment

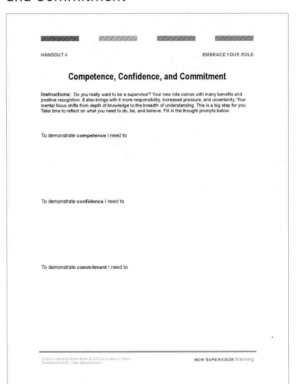

Handout 5: Promote Communication

HANDOUT 5   PROMOTE COMMUNICATION

Promote Communication

Instructions: Although this workshop is not about communication, communication skills are a basic requirement for being a good supervisor. Examine the graph below with a partner and then answer the questions that follow.

Feedback: Manager Versus Employee Perceptions

Employees receive sufficient feedback or advice on areas in which they need improvement.
- Managers Agree 89%
- Employees Agree 57%

Employees receive sufficient feedback or advice on how to maximize their strengths.
- Managers Agree 82%
- Employees Agree 49%

Note: Data from a DDI Survey of 1,800 managers and 1,800 employees from over 200 companies.

Source: R. Smith and M. Campbell, *Talent Conversations* (Greensboro, NC: Center for Creative Leadership, 2011).

How do you interpret this information?

Think back to before you became a supervisor. Does this seem accurate? In other forms of communication too?

What implications does this have for you as a supervisor?

Original material by Elaine Biech. © 2015 Association for Talent Development (ATD). Used with permission.   **NEW SUPERVISOR** training

---

Handout 6: Share What You Know

HANDOUT 6   PROMOTE COMMUNICATION

Share What You Know

Instructions: Let's take a few minutes to review how much you already know about communication and what will be important to remember as a supervisor. In your small group defined by your facilitator, list recommendations for your assigned communication topic on this handout. Then capture your group's insights on the appropriate flipchart in the room.

Clear Communication

Active Listening

Influencing Others Based on Communication Style (DiSC, MBTI, or others)

Facilitating Effective Meetings

"The day soldiers stop bringing you their problems is the day you have stopped leading them."
—General Colin Powell

Original material by Elaine Biech. © 2015 Association for Talent Development (ATD). Used with permission.   **NEW SUPERVISOR** training

---

Handout 7: Guide the Work—With a 21st-Century Caveat

HANDOUT 7   GUIDE THE WORK

Guide the Work—with a 21st Century Caveat

Four functions of management define the role of supervisors and managers in a business environment:

- **Plan:** Decide upon business goals and the methods to achieve them.
- **Organize:** Determine the best allocation of people and resources.
- **Direct/Lead:** Motivate, instruct, and supervise workers assigned to the activity.
- **Control:** Establish performance standards, analyze metrics during activities, ensure completion of tasks, and identify areas for improvement.

At times, "staffing" is also included as an important management practice. Without people, no organization can do business. Done right, staffing puts the right person in the right job, which becomes an ongoing activity as employees change jobs. Together, these five practices are the requirements to complete any work and get it out the door.

Today's workplace, however, requires much more to ensure employees are engaged. Fostering engagement requires that you involve employees to the greatest extent in planning and organizing the work; invite them to share ideas and put decision making in their hands; and clarify roles, provide support, remove barriers, and facilitate employees' ability to reach the goal. Supervisors motivate and develop employees to ensure they have the necessary skills and knowledge, and they must delegate the right tasks to the right people. And, finally, control should also encourage individual responsibility and accountability. All of this requires crystal clear communication and active listening.

A supervisor's role is more demanding than ever in a VUCA (volatile, uncertain, complex, and ambiguous) world. Our organizations operate under the conditions defined as a VUCA world, and these same conditions will complicate your ability to supervise. You will be expected to make decisions and solve problems quickly. Therefore, your employees need to be fully engaged.

Original material by Elaine Biech. © 2015 Association for Talent Development (ATD). Used with permission.   **NEW SUPERVISOR** training

---

Handout 8a: Eggs-perience a Supervisor's Job: Management Functions

HANDOUT 8A   GUIDE THE WORK

Eggs-perience a Supervisor's Job: Management Functions

Based on your "eggs-perience," identify additional recommendations for each of the four management functions. You may use any resources in the room or online that you wish.

Plan	Organize
• Communicate and involve	• Communicate and delegate
• Get employees excited and energized	• Set schedules to meet goals
• Identify and tap into individual strengths	• Identify and review milestones
• Don't wait for perfection or all the information to make decisions	• Involve your team for all reorganization
• Support the organization's decisions/direction	• Clarify roles and delegate authority
	• Seek ideas and consensus

Lead	Control
• Communicate and motivate	• Communicate and celebrate achievements
• Be available for questions and develop	• Compare results to goal
• Provide guidance and support	• Identify lessons learned
• Inspire action and empower your team	• Find ways to improve repeated processes
• Expect individual accountability	• Examine organizational, budgetary, market, HR, and information controls for future tasks
• Take time to reward and recognize	

Original material by Elaine Biech. © 2015 Association for Talent Development (ATD). Used with permission.   **NEW SUPERVISOR** training

Handout 8b: Eggs-perience a Supervisor's Job: Delegation

Eggs-perience a Supervisor's Job: Delegation

Delegation is the process of transferring responsibility and decision-making authority from a supervisor to an employee. It is the best time management tool at your disposal and, even more important, helps others develop and grow. Successfully delegated assignments help employees gain confidence, expand job capabilities, and give them a chance to demonstrate their potential. Delegation builds trust, motivation, and strong teams.

Successful delegation must be accompanied by an assigned level of authority. Too little authority limits the choices the employee can make; too much authority can make supervisors uneasy about the potential for costly mistakes. The solution is to determine the appropriate level of authority before assigning the task.

Instructions: Define the characteristics and expectations for each level of authority.

No Authority

The supervisor

The employee

Medium Authority

The supervisor

The employee

Complete Authority

The supervisor

The employee

How did authority come into play during the ESP Project? What would you do differently?

Handout 8b, *continued*

When to Delegate?

Use this decision framework to help you determine when to delegate.

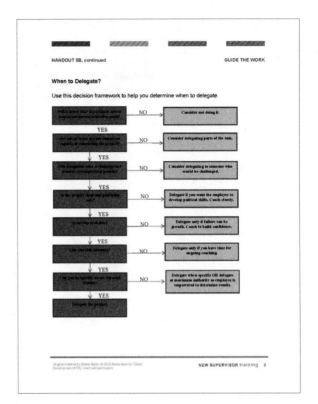

Handout 8b, *continued*

Delegation Process

1. Communicate the project, describing exactly what and when it needs to be done.
2. Explain why the task needs to be done and how it fits into the bigger picture.
3. Agree on the standards you will use to measure success.
4. Grant authority and clarify parameters.
5. Provide support and resources.
6. Get commitment and confirm your employee understands.

Select the Right Person	Delegation Tips for Success
• Who is qualified and available? • Who can be trained? • Who will benefit in terms of development? • Who will be motivated? • Who will accept the planned authority level?	• Delegate the whole project to one person. • Clearly specify your preferred results. • Assign the project, not the method. • Ask employees for their ideas and input. • Reward results.

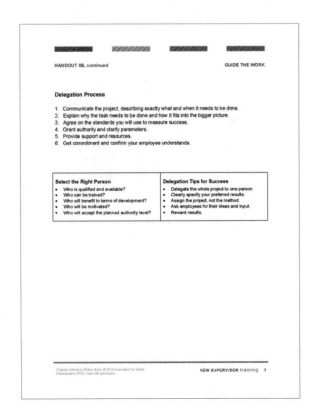

Handout 8c: Eggs-perience a Supervisor's Job: Making Decisions and Solving Problems

Eggs-perience a Supervisor's Job: Making Decisions and Solving Problems

Instructions: How involved in decisions were each of you during the ESP Project? Share your thoughts with the group.

What is the result of including others in decision making on the job?

Identify ways that supervisors can involve employees when making decisions.

This seven-step process works well for making decisions and solving problems. Add your ideas.

1. Identify the decision or issue.
   • Is it worth investing time?
   •
2. Gather information and learn others' interests.
   • What's relevant to know before making the decision?
   •
3. Analyze the situation.
   • What alternatives exist?
   •
4. Develop options or alternatives.
   • How many options can you generate? Ask "what if" questions.
   •
5. Evaluate the options.
   • What criteria will you used to evaluate?
   •
6. Select the preferred option.
   • What risks and problems might this decision create?
   •
7. Implement the plan.
   • Do you have commitment and resources for the plan?
   •

> Do not procrastinate. If you have enough of what you need to make a decision, make it.

Handout 8d: Eggs-perience a Supervisor's Job: Process Improvement & Managing Change

Eggs-perience a Supervisor's Job: Process Improvement and Managing Change

Process Improvement

Process improvement is the proactive approach of identifying, analyzing, and improving your department's processes. There are many approaches and methodologies. Which ones have you used? Draw your own model here explaining what might occur in each step and why continuous process improvement is important to your role as a supervisor.

Managing Change

How did you feel when team members were moved to a different team?

What would have made this more acceptable?

How does moving team members relate to your real work world?

What do you recommend to supervisors when they know a change will affect their departments?

Handout 9: What's Engagement Got to Do With It?

What's Engagement Got to Do With It?

You've probably heard discussions about engagement, but what is it, why is it important, and why should you care? It would seem that you have enough on your mind as you move into a new role as a supervisor. So what's engagement got to do with it?

There are multiple definitions for "employee engagement," but the one that most organizations seem to adopt is "the capture of discretionary effort." Discretionary effort results when employees go beyond ordinary expectations to get the job done. The Conference Board defines employee engagement as "a heightened emotional connection that an employee feels for his or her organization that influences him or her to exert greater discretionary effort to the work." It occurs because employees believe that they and the organization are mutually supporting each other to meet their separate goals.

But what leads to engagement? Dozens of employee engagement studies have been published since 2000 by top research firms such as Gallup, Towers Perrin, Hewitt Associates, Blessing White, the Corporate Leadership Council, and others. Each of the studies used different definitions that resulted in at least 26 key drivers of engagement. Some studies, for example, emphasized the underlying cognitive issues; others emphasized the underlying emotional issues. More than half of the studies agreed on these eight key drivers:

- **Trust and integrity.** How well do managers communicate and "walk the talk"?
- **Nature of the job.** Is the job mentally stimulating day-to-day?
- **Connection of employee performance to organizational performance.** Do employees understand how their work contributes to the organization's performance?
- **Career growth.** Are future opportunities for growth abundant?
- **Pride about the organization.** How much self-esteem do employees feel by being associated with their organization?
- **Co-workers/team members.** How much do relationships influence one's level of engagement?
- **Employee development.** Is the organization making an effort to develop individuals' skills?
- **Relationship with one's manager.** Do employees value their relationships with their managers?

Handout 9, *continued*

Key findings include the fact that larger companies are more challenged to engage employees than smaller companies. Also, employee age drives a clear difference in the importance of some drivers. For example, employees under the age of 44 rank "challenging environment/career growth opportunities" much higher than do older employees, who value "recognition and reward for their contributions" (Conference Board 2006). But all studies, all locations, and all ages agreed that the direct relationship with one's manager is the strongest of all drivers.

And that is why you should care.

You may wonder whether employee engagement is just another trend or really significant. Employee engagement is very significant to organizational success. There is clear evidence that high levels of engagement correlate to individual, group, and corporate performance in areas such as retention, turnover, productivity, customer service, and loyalty. And this is not just by small margins. Differences vary between studies, but in all cases highly engaged employees outperform their disengaged counterparts in many areas.

A 2012 Gallup study, "Engagement at Work: Its Effect on Performance Continues in Tough Economic Times," which examined 50,000 organizations and about 1.4 million employees in 192 organizations in 34 countries, presents a strong business case for increasing employee engagement. The study measured the difference between the top 25 and the bottom 25 percent of engaged employees and found that organizations with the most engaged employees

- Have 37 percent lower absenteeism
- Experienced 25 to 65 percent lower turnover
- Experienced 48 percent fewer safety incidents
- Have 41 percent fewer quality issues
- Have 10 percent higher customer satisfaction
- Deliver 21 percent higher productivity for the organization
- Enjoy 22 percent higher profitability.

How does this happen? There is not just one thing you can do. There is no "program" to increase employee engagement. Engagement starts with your organization, but it is most dependent upon supervisors. It encompasses everything that you do. Review the eight key drivers and list how you could influence them positively by what you do or don't do.

Handout 9, *continued*

KEY DRIVERS	DO	DON'T
Trust and integrity		
Nature of the job		
Connection to organization performance		
Career growth opportunities		
Pride about the organization		
Co-workers/team members		
Employee development		
Relationship with one's manager		

Sources: Conference Board, "Employee Engagement: A Review of Current Research and Its Implications" (New York: Conference Board, 2006); and Gallup, "Engagement at Work: Its Effect on Performance Continues in Tough Economic Times" (Washington, DC: Gallup, 2012).

Handout 10: Hire the Right Employee

Hire the Right Employee

Hiring new employees may be one of the most important decisions you make as a supervisor. It takes time, but the investment is worth it. Hiring a good fit to your organization and department will pay back in working with someone who has a positive attitude, accomplishes critical goals, enhances department morale, and builds camaraderie in your organization. These suggestions can help you locate and hire the best candidate. What can you do to build on the suggestions?

TO HIRE THE BEST	WHAT I COULD IMPROVE
Clearly define the job as the foundation; update a current job description.	
Review current recruiting; use social media; check out your company's recruitment site.	
Review applications carefully; ask how they stack up to desired characteristics.	
Prescreen candidates to save interviewing time.	
Ask interview questions that find the best candidates; use behavioral questions.	
Always check backgrounds and references before making a job offer.	

Interview questions should focus on the foundational needs you identified when you defined the job description. Besides the experience and skills, what is important to the job? What motivates the candidate? Is there a culture fit? How good is the person's communication? Behavioral-type questions help you reach these needs. The examples here are just a few of the thousands of good interviewing questions on the Internet:

- Describe the work environment in which you are most productive and happy.
- Describe your leadership style. How do you communicate?
- What goals, including career goals, have you set for your life?
- How would you define *success* for your career?
- Tell us about a colleague with whom you have had difficulty working? What did you do about it?
- What contributions did you make to your current or past employer of which you are most proud?

What are your favorite interviewing questions?

Handout 11: Orient New Employees

Orient New Employees

Instructions: Orientation isn't an event; it's a process that starts before the first day the employee begins to work for your organization. Your organization has an orientation process, but as the supervisor you also have responsibilities. Use this checklist to effectively assimilate new hires.

Pre-Start
- ☐ Call to congratulate your newest employee.
- ☐ Offer support, information, and help.
- ☐ Schedule your welcome meeting on the first day.
- ☐ Inform others in the department of the new hire's start date.
- ☐ Ensure the new employee's workspace is set up prior arrival.

First Day/Week
- ☐ Introduce your new employee to others in the department.
- ☐ Allow time to set up workspace.
- ☐ Introduce your new employee to a peer mentor.
- ☐ Schedule time for a review of your organization's intranet.
- ☐ Add new hire to relevant distribution lists.
- ☐ At the end of the week review the activities and ask about needs.

First Month
- ☐ Meet with your new employee weekly to address goals, training, performance expectations, and key corporate topics.
- ☐ Introduce your new employee to senior management.
- ☐ Check with the peer mentor and offer your support.
- ☐ Review your new hire's workload and schedule regular progress updates.

First Three Months
- ☐ Continue to conduct weekly meetings addressing goals and IDP planning.
- ☐ Create opportunities for cross-division and cross-department contacts.
- ☐ Ensure the employee has exposure to a variety of projects and learning opportunities.
- ☐ Provide an informal review of performance to date and discuss developmental needs.

Three to Six Months
- ☐ Continue meeting to discuss goals, development, training, and other updates.
- ☐ Recognize and celebrate accomplishments for the first six months.
- ☐ Provide a formal performance review.

> "To win in the marketplace you must first win in the workplace."
> —Doug Conant
> CEO of Campbell's Soup

Handout 12: Develop Individuals

Develop Individuals

Assist Employees to Set Career Goals

Engaged employees feel a sense of achievement and satisfaction in their work. Development goals that focus on their careers increase satisfaction and help them plan for the future. Show your staff how the goals relate to the organization. Ask questions such as these to help them focus on appropriate goals:

- What would you like your next position to be? How do you think you can best work toward reaching that position? What do you need to learn? What experiences would be helpful?
- What long-range goals have you set for yourself? Where do you see yourself in ten years?
- How is your present job preparing you for the goals you have set for yourself?
- What do you know about the requirements for the goals you have set for yourself? What do you still need to learn about the position you would like to have?
- What do you feel would be helpful for your job or career development? What experiences or training do you need to be more productive or successful?
- What changes must you make to reach the goals you are setting? Can they be made within the boundaries of your present position?

Use a Career Goal Grid to Help Improve Skills

This career goal grid can help you guide employees in setting objective, attainable goals based on the answers to four key questions:

- What do you want that you don't do? (Start)
- What do you want that you already do? (Continue)
- What don't you do that you don't want to do? (Avoid)
- What do you do now that you want to stop doing? (Stop)

	Start	**Continue**
	Avoid	**Stop**

Do you want to do it? (Yes / No) — Do you do it now? (Yes)

Handout 12, *continued*

Using an IDP to Plan Employees' Development

Individual development plans (IDPs) provide a blueprint for each employee and are especially useful to record and track goals, identify developmental strategies, and document accomplishments. They generally identify long- and short-term plans and provide an opportunity for supervisors to add their comments and support.

In addition to establishing performance goals and objectives, IDPs also emphasize opportunities for employees to learn and grow. An IDP compliments an employee's goals and objectives, tying personal development to the organization's goals.

A mid-year review of the IDP may coincide with a mid-year performance review as long as there is a clear distinction between performance and development. The employee and supervisor should review the IDP at the end of the performance year before drafting the next year's IDP. Consider these suggestions for creating effective IDPs:

- Create IDPs with input from both you (the supervisor) and the employee.
- Outline plans that challenge employees based on their strengths, development needs, and career aspirations.
- Provide opportunities for supervisor and employee discussions.
- Identify ways to leverage strengths and to improve development areas.
- Focus on no more than one or two general areas where the employee needs to improve.
- Include development goals that are achievable and measurable.
- Develop a plan of action with associated timelines that assist the employee to achieve the goals.
- Ensure that as the supervisor you have the ability to help the employee gain necessary development opportunities and skills.
- Include informal and formal training options that align with the employee's interests and goals.
- Include ideas for "stretch assignments" for the employee.
- Maintain IDPs as living documents that reflect changes in employees' situations and skills.
- Incorporate both long- and short-term goals.
- Review IDPs several times each year.

What value do IDPs provide to you as the supervisor?

> "Life is about getting A's—not some normal distribution curve. Managers need to spend less time evaluating employees and more time helping them succeed."
> —Garry Ridge
> CEO, WD-40 Company

Handout 13: Foster Teamwork

Handout 14: It Won't All Be Easy

Handout 14, *continued*

Handout 15: Establish a Motivating Environment

Handout 16: Five-Step Employee Performance Process

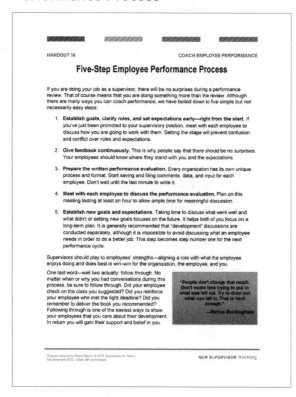

Handout 17: Goals, Roles, and Expectations

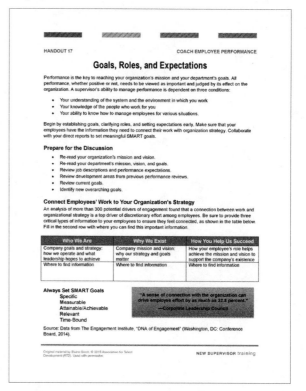

Handout 18: Continuous Feedback

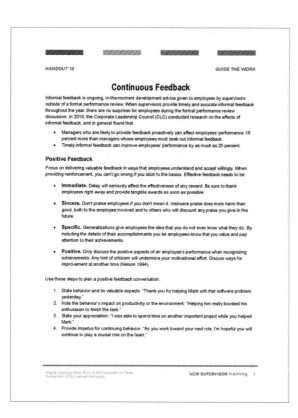

Handout 18, *continued*

Handout 19: Conduct Effective Performance Reviews

HANDOUT 19 — COACH EMPLOYEE PERFORMANCE

Conduct Effective Performance Reviews

Employees typically report dissatisfaction with their performance management feedback. When executed well, delivering performance reviews that focus on the right type of feedback can impact employee performance by more than 25 percent, according to the *Harvard Business Review*. The formal review is a balance of positive and developmental feedback. Keep in mind these tips to increase your effectiveness in delivering performance reviews:

- Practice what you will say prior to the meeting.
- Plan for enough time when you will not be disturbed.
- Give the employee a copy of the performance review.
- Start with strengths before discussing development areas.
- Concentrate on employee behaviors, not personality traits.
- Offer examples of the changes that are required.
- Use clear and simple language during the discussion.
- Listen, listen, listen; aim for a 50/50 discussion.
- Tie improvement ideas to the employee's strengths when possible.
- Provide suggestions for how performance could be improved.
- Ask for questions or comments throughout.
- Obtain the employee's commitment to meet all objectives by the date you've agreed.
- Discuss next steps for both you and the employee.
- End with a positive comment.

Do Use These Language Tips
- ☑ Use the term *development* when discussing improvement needs.
- ☑ Use positive, empathetic sentences.
- ☑ Use examples that can be seen or heard.
- ☑ Provide encouragement.

Don't Make These Faux Pas
- ☒ Don't make value judgements or comparisons.
- ☒ Don't use words such as *always, never, best, bad, weaknesses*.
- ☒ Don't label the employee as *irresponsible or poor performer*.
- ☒ Don't apologize after delivering required improvement feedback.

Source: Data from Harvard HBR, *Analytic Service Report* (Cambridge, MA: Harvard Business Review, 2013).

Original material by Elaine Biech, © 2015 Association for Talent Development (ATD). Used with permission. **NEW SUPERVISOR** training

Handout 20: Feedback Practice

HANDOUT 20 — COACH EMPLOYEE PERFORMANCE

Feedback Practice

Instructions: Here's a chance to practice giving feedback:

1. Select one of the scenarios below. Choose one that is similar to a situation you may be facing now or have in the past.
2. Take 3 minutes to make a few notes at the bottom of this page.
3. Select a partner and a place where you can practice.
4. Decide who will give (the supervisor) and who will receive (the employee) the feedback first. The supervisor takes a minute to set the stage. Employees, be realistic, ask questions, and use the content in Handouts 18 and 19 as a basis of feedback to the "supervisor."
5. Your facilitator will tell you when to begin. You will have 5 minute to practice. At the end of 5 minutes, the facilitator will call time and the "employee" will take another 5 minutes to give feedback.
6. Change roles and repeat steps 4 and 5.

Scenarios. Choose one or use one of your own.

Situation 1: You are conducting a performance review of a person you know could be doing better. The employee acts shocked that you are questioning his/her performance. How do you respond?

Situation 2: You have an employee who is unfocused. He/she tends to socialize more than appropriate and is starting to bother other employees. What feedback do you provide?

Situation 3: One of your employees is a doomsday naysayer. This employee is productive but upsets everyone by spreading rumors and complaining about everything. What feedback do you give?

Situation 4: One of your employees is often a little late completing assigned tasks. It hasn't affected the results to date, but it annoys others in the department. What do you say?

Situation 5: One of the few females in your department has been falling behind. You have faith that she can do the job, but when you called her into your office and state your concerns she burst into tears. What do you do?

NOTES

_____
_____
_____
_____
_____

Original material by Elaine Biech, © 2015 Association for Talent Development (ATD). Used with permission. **NEW SUPERVISOR** training

Handout 21: Negative Feedback Isn't Fun

HANDOUT 21 — COACH EMPLOYEE PERFORMANCE

Negative Feedback Isn't Fun

Your employees want the negative feedback you hate to give. Yep! That's right! Think about it. Would you rather have positive feedback about your performance or suggestions for improvement? A January 2014 post by Jack Zenger on his Harvard Business Review blog reports that Zenger | Folkman collected data from 899 individuals—49 percent from the United States and the remainder from abroad—to address this very question.

They found that people want corrective feedback more than praise—if it's provided in a constructive manner. By a three to one margin, respondents reported they believe it does more to improve their performance than positive feedback. When asked what was most helpful in their careers, 72 percent thought their performance would improve if their managers would provide corrective feedback. But how it is conducted is also important. It should be provided in a thoughtful, caring, helpful spirit.

What Else Do Your Employees Want?

Lore International Institute surveyed employees from many types of industries and found that what employees want isn't unreasonable: honesty, fairness, trust, and respect. Here are more of their suggestions (Bacon 2006):

- **Treat employees like human beings.** Learn their names and use them. Celebrate their birthdays and their triumphs. Learn a few details about them, their interests, and their families. Write the information down to help you remember if you must.
- **A penny for your thoughts.** Ask people for ideas. Then identify the best, act on them, and give credit to the employees.
- **Offer risky projects.** Trust people with "stretch" assignments even if the outcome is uncertain. This is their chance to shine. If they fall short, they will grow and perhaps learn even more from the experience.
- **Support through thick and thin.** Some projects start off strong and wind up failing. Show your employees you've got their backs and help them regroup and recover when the going gets tough.
- **Pay attention.** Don't make your electronics more important than your employees. Turn off the phone, stop emailing, and meet people face-to-face with no distractions.
- **Keep secrets.** Respect what people tell you in confidence. Unless a secret crosses a legal or ethical line, keep it to yourself.

Who Do You Want to Retain?

Think of an employee you want to retain. What do you think he or she wants from you? How well have you been delivering on the expectation? What could you do better?

Source: Suggestions adapted from T. Bacon, *What People Want* (Mountain View, CA: Davies-Black, 2006).

Original material by Elaine Biech, © 2015 Association for Talent Development (ATD). Used with permission. **NEW SUPERVISOR** training

Handout 22: Rewards, Recognition, and Retention

HANDOUT 22 — COACH EMPLOYEE PERFORMANCE

Rewards, Recognition, and Retention

Retaining the best employees and talent is critical to a company's success. A supervisor's ability to reward and recognize achievement effectively can increase employees' discretionary effort and intent to stay. How can you make recognition most effective?

- **Link rewards to organizational goals.** Reward an action or behavior that links to the organization's mission, vision, and values. Reward an action or behavior that helps the team accomplish its goals.
- **Involve employee preferences.** Ensure that the recognition is meaningful to the employee. When possible tailor recognition based on what motivates the employee.
- **Communicate recognition.** Champion the accomplishments of your employees to others. Communicate rewards to your team to provide recognition for performance or promotion.
- **Recognize relevant actions.** Recognize actions and behaviors that are important to your team and the organization. Explain the reasons for recognizing a particular action or behavior.
- **Reward in a timely manner.** Give recognition close to when the behavior or action occurs to clearly link the behavior and the result.

Ideas for Rewards and Recognition

Public Acknowledgement
Token of Appreciation
Development Opportunities
Low-Cost Perks

Original material by Elaine Biech, © 2015 Association for Talent Development (ATD). Used with permission. **NEW SUPERVISOR** training

Chapter 13: **Handouts**   167

Handout 23: Retain Your Best

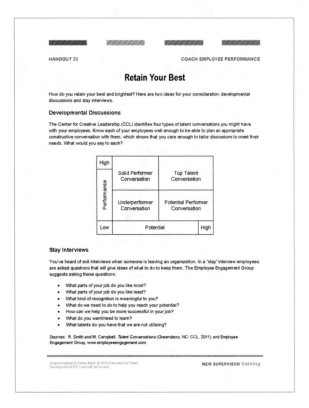

Handout 24: How Do You Model Excellence?

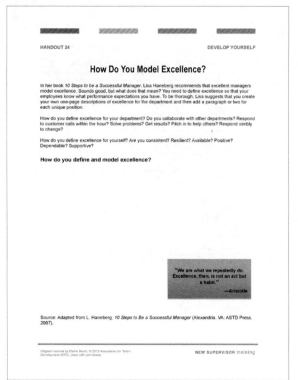

Handout 25: Manage Your Time

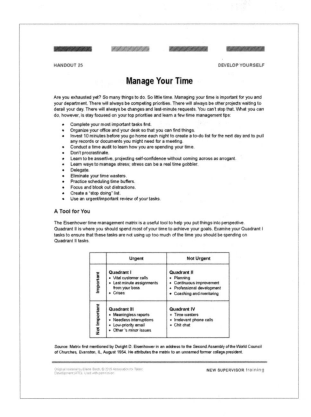

Handout 26: Get Better All the Time: Your Professional Development

Handout 26, *continued*

HANDOUT 26, continued — DEVELOP YOURSELF

How to Learn?

- Seek feedback
- Ask questions
- Ask for guidance and assistance
- Ask your supervisor, peers, and subordinates for ideas
- Regularly solicit feedback from others about your management skills
- Find a mentor
- Hire a personal or professional coach
- Read articles and books on management
- Practice management skills out of the office
- Learn to be a mentor
- Learn to coach others
- Give a presentation
- Join Toastmasters or another speaking group
- Practice basic skills in delegation
- Practice basic skills in listening and sharing feedback
- Customize personal guidelines for problem solving, decision making, or planning
- Plan and facilitate a meeting
- Volunteer to lead a work or community project, or join a board of directors
- Maintain a journal
- Identify traits and behaviors of your favorite managers—and then emulate them
- Sign up for a course, apprenticeship, or internship
- Take a leadership or management role in an association

> "People don't plan to fail; they fail to plan."
> —John Beckley
> First Librarian of the U.S. Congress

Handout 27: Develop Your Personal Leadership Guiding Beliefs

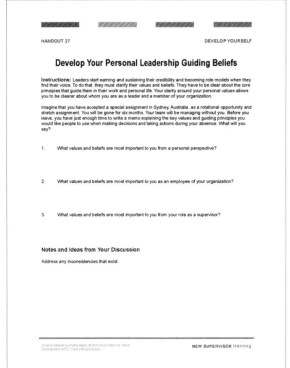

HANDOUT 27 — DEVELOP YOURSELF

Develop Your Personal Leadership Guiding Beliefs

Instructions: Leaders start earning and sustaining their credibility and becoming role models when they find their voice. To do that, they must clarify their values and beliefs. They have to be clear about the core principles that guide them in their work and personal life. Your clarity around your personal values allows you to be clearer about whom you are as a leader and a member of your organization.

Imagine that you have accepted a special assignment in Sydney, Australia, as a rotational opportunity and stretch assignment. You will be gone for six months. Your team will be managing without you. Before you leave, you have just enough time to write a memo explaining the key values and guiding principles you would like people to use when making decisions and taking actions during your absence. What will you say?

1. What values and beliefs are most important to you from a personal perspective?

2. What values and beliefs are most important to you as an employee of your organization?

3. What values and beliefs are most important to you from your role as a supervisor?

Notes and Ideas from Your Discussion

Address any inconsistencies that exist.

Handout 28: Action Planning: My Next Steps

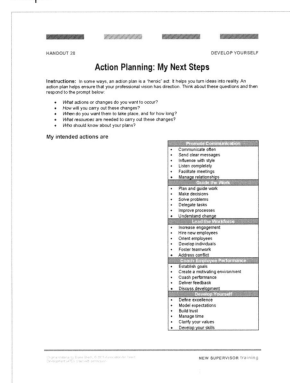

HANDOUT 28 — DEVELOP YOURSELF

Action Planning: My Next Steps

Instructions: In some ways, an action plan is a "heroic" act: It helps you turn ideas into reality. An action plan helps ensure that your professional vision has direction. Think about these questions and then respond to the prompt below:

- *What* actions or changes do you want to occur?
- *How* will you carry out these changes?
- *When* do you want them to take place, and for how long?
- *What* resources are needed to carry out these changes?
- *Who* should know about your plans?

My intended actions are

Promote Communication
- Communicate often
- Send clear messages
- Influence with style
- Listen completely
- Facilitate meetings
- Manage relationships

Guide the Work
- Plan and guide work
- Make decisions
- Solve problems
- Delegate tasks
- Improve processes
- Understand change

Lead the Workforce
- Increase engagement
- Hire new employees
- Orient employees
- Develop individuals
- Foster teamwork
- Address conflict

Coach Employee Performance
- Establish goals
- Create a motivating environment
- Coach performance
- Deliver feedback
- Discuss development

Develop Yourself
- Define excellence
- Model expectations
- Build trust
- Manage time
- Clarify your values
- Develop your skills

Handout 29: What Do Great Supervisors Do Every Day?

HANDOUT 29 — DEVELOP YOURSELF

What Do Great Supervisors Do Every Day?

It is never too early to start good habits. As you move into your supervisory role begin to think about how you will demonstrate that you are a GREAT SUPERVISOR.

What do great supervisors do every day?

- Improve their communication skills.
- Get to know their people; be interested in them.
- Deliver feedback continuously.
- Reinforce those who do what's expected.
- Encourage an innovative, accepting atmosphere.
- Encourage an innovative environment.
- Keep their employees informed.
- Keep their bosses informed.
- Solicit feedback.
- Partner risks with their staff.
- Are personable, approachable, and positive.
- Make timely decisions.
- Tackle difficult issues immediately.
- Address nonperformance immediately.

Now, as a great supervisor, what will YOU do every day?

Handout 30: Reading List for Your Continued Development

Reading List for Your Continued Development

Biech, E. (2010). *The ASTD Leadership Handbook.* Alexandria, VA: ASTD Press.

Blanchard, K., and S. Johnson. (2003). *The One-Minute Manager.* New York: William Morrow.

Haneberg, L. (2007). *10 Steps to Be a Successful Manager.* Alexandria, VA: ASTD Press.

Haneberg, L. (2008). *Developing Great Managers.* Alexandria, VA: ASTD Press.

Hersey, P. (1992). *The Situational Leader.* Cary, NC: Center for Leadership Studies.

Kaye, B. (2012). *Help Them Grow or Watch Them Go.* San Francisco: Berrett-Koehler.

Kelleher, Bob. (2014). *Employee Engagement for Dummies.* Hoboken, NJ: Wiley.

Nelson, Bob. (2012). *1501 Ways to Reward Employees.* New York: Workman.

Original material by Elaine Biech. © 2015 Association for Talent Development (ATD). Used with permission.

NEW SUPERVISOR training

Chapter 14

Online Tools and Downloads

What's in This Chapter

- Instructions to access supporting materials
- Options for using tools and downloads
- Licensing and copyright information for workshop programs
- Tips for working with the downloaded files

The ATD Workshop Series is designed to give you flexible options for many levels of training facilitation and topic expertise. As you prepare your program, you will want to incorporate many of the handouts, assessments, presentation slides, and other training tools provided as supplementary materials with this volume. We wish you the best of luck in delivering your training workshops. It is exciting work that ultimately can change lives.

Access to Free Supporting Materials

To get started, visit the ATD Workshop Series page: www.td.org/workshopbooks. This page includes links to download all the free supporting materials that accompany this book, as well as up-to-date information about additions to the series and new program offerings.

These downloads, which are included in the price of the book, feature ready-to-use learning activities, handouts, assessments, and presentation slide files in PDF format. Use these files to deliver your workshop program and as a resource to help you prepare your own materials. You may download and use any of these files as part of your training delivery for the workshops, provided no changes are made to the original materials. To access this material, you will be asked to log into the ATD website. If you are not an ATD member, you will have to create an ATD account.

If you choose to re-create these documents, they can only be used within your organization; they cannot be presented or sold as your original work. Please note that all materials included in the book are copyrighted and you are using them with permission of ATD. If you choose to re-create the materials, per copyright usage requirements, you must provide attribution to the original source of the content and display a copyright notice as follows:

© 2015 ATD. Adapted and used with permission.

Customizable Materials

You can also choose to customize this supporting content for an additional licensing fee. This option gives you access to a downloadable zip file with the entire collection of supporting materials in Microsoft Word and PowerPoint file formats. Once purchased, you will have indefinite and unlimited access to these materials through the My Downloads section of your ATD account. Then, you will be able to customize and personalize all the documents and presentations using Microsoft Word and PowerPoint. You can add your own content, change the order or format, include your company logo, or make any other customization.

Please note that all the original documents contain attribution to ATD and this book as the original source for the material. As you customize the documents, remember to keep these attributions intact (see the copyright notice above). By doing so, you are practicing professional courtesy by respecting the intellectual property rights of another trainer (the author) and modeling respect for copyright and intellectual property laws for your program participants.

ATD offers two custom material license options: Internal Use and Client Use. To determine which license option you need to purchase, ask yourself the following question:

Will I or my employer be charging a person or outside organization a fee for providing services or for delivering training that includes any ATD Workshop content that you wish to customize?

If the answer is yes, then you need to purchase a Client Use license.

If the answer is no, and you plan to customize ATD Workshop content to deliver training at no cost to employees within your own department or company only, you need to purchase the Internal Use license.

Working With the Files

PDF Documents

To read or print the PDF files you download, you must have PDF reader software such as Adobe Acrobat Reader installed on your system. The program can be downloaded free of cost from the Adobe website: www.adobe.com. To print documents, simply use the PDF reader to open the downloaded files and print as many copies as you need.

PowerPoint Slides

To use or adapt the contents of the PowerPoint presentation files (available with the Internal Use and Client Use licenses), you must have Microsoft PowerPoint software installed on your system. If you simply want to view the PowerPoint documents, you only need an appropriate viewer on your system. Microsoft provides various viewers for free download at www.microsoft.com.

Once you have downloaded the files to your computer system, use Microsoft PowerPoint (or free viewer) to print as many copies of the presentation slides as you need. You can also make handouts of the presentations by choosing the "print three slides per page" option on the print menu.

You can modify or otherwise customize the slides by opening and editing them in Microsoft PowerPoint. However, you must retain the credit line denoting the original source of the material, as noted earlier in this chapter. It is illegal to present this content as your own work. The files will open as read-only files, so before you adapt them you will need to save them onto your hard drive. Furthermore, use of the images in the slides for any purpose other than presenting the workshops in this book is strictly prohibited by law.

The PowerPoint slides included in this volume support the three workshop agendas:

- Two-Day Workshop
- One-Day Workshop
- Half-Day Workshop

For PowerPoint slides to successfully support and augment your learning program, it is essential that you practice giving presentations with the slides *before* using them in live training situations. You should be confident that you can logically expand on the points featured in the presentations and discuss the methods for working through them. If you want to fully engage your participants, become familiar with this technology before you use it. See the text box that follows for a cheat sheet to help you navigate through the presentation. A good practice is to insert comments into PowerPoint's notes feature, which you can print out and use when you present the slides. The workshop agendas in this book show thumbnails of each slide to help you keep your place as you deliver the workshop.

NAVIGATING THROUGH A POWERPOINT PRESENTATION	
Key	**PowerPoint "Show" Action**
Space bar or Enter or Mouse click	Advance through custom animations embedded in the presentation
Backspace	Back up to the last projected element of the presentation
Escape	Abort the presentation
B or b	Blank the screen to black
B or b (repeat)	Resume the presentation
W or w	Blank the screen to white
W or w (repeat)	Resume the presentation

Acknowledgments

This volume draws heavily upon what I've learned from the professionals in the organizations that allow me to experiment with leadership, supervision, change, and a potpourri of other topics. I enjoy working with you, and it is so much fun when we triumph over huge hurdles. My humble thanks to all of you. You motivate me.

Thank you to all the supervisors out there doing a yeoman's job to keep your organizations running smoothly.

I am grateful to my husband, Dan, who created masterpieces in the kitchen to sustain me through all those long hours of writing: cinnamon chip scones, brandied onion soup, tarragon turkey salad, cherry-glazed pork chops, portabella parmesan, and stuffed acorn squash. Mmmmmmm.

Thank you to everyone at ATD and TPH who makes me look good: Cat Russo, divine friend and publisher, for reviving this series and inviting me to share in the fun; Jacki Edlund-Braun, editor extraordinaire who prods prepositions into place, cuts contrary commas, reduces redundancy, and selects precisely the right words; Tora Estep, who understands me and my idiosyncrasies, partnering to fill the gaps as if I'd done it myself; Tony Bingham, who allows me to continue to play in the fabulous ATD world; and the whole team at ATD Press.

About the Author

Elaine Biech, president of ebb associates inc, a strategic implementation, leadership development, and experiential learning consulting firm, has been in the field more than 30 years helping organizations work through large-scale change. She has presented at dozens of national and international conferences and has been featured in publications such as the *Wall Street Journal, Harvard Management Update, Investor's Business Daily,* and *Fortune.* She is the author and editor of more than 60 books, receiving national awards for two of them.

Among her extensive body of published work are many ATD titles, including ASTD's flagship publication *The ASTD Handbook: The Definitive Reference for Training & Development* (editor, 2014). Other ATD/ASTD titles include *The Book of Road-Tested Activities* (co-published with Pfeiffer, 2011); *ASTD Leadership Handbook* (2010); *ASTD's Ultimate Train the Trainer* (2009); *10 Steps to Successful Training* (2009); *ASTD Handbook for Workplace Learning Professionals* (2008); and *Thriving Through Change: A Leader's Practical Guide to Change Mastery* (2007), to name just a few.

Elaine specializes in helping leaders maximize their effectiveness. Customizing all of her work for individual clients, she conducts strategic planning sessions and implements corporate-wide systems such as quality improvement, change management, reengineering of business processes, and mentoring programs. Elaine is a consummate training professional, facilitating training on a wide range of workplace and business topics. She is particularly adept at turning dysfunctional teams into productive teams.

As a management consultant, trainer, and designer, she has provided services globally to organizations as diverse as Outback Steakhouse, Johnson Wax, FAA, Land O' Lakes, McDonald's, Lands' End, General Casualty Insurance, Chrysler, Johnson Wax, Federal Reserve Bank, China Sinopec, PricewaterhouseCoopers, Banco de Credito Peru, Minera Yanacocha, Newmont Mining, American Family Insurance, Hershey Chocolate, U.S. Navy, NASA, Newport News Shipbuilding, Kohler Company, ASTD, American Red Cross, Association of Independent Certified Public Accountants, the University of Wisconsin, The College of William and Mary, Old

Dominion University, and hundreds of other public and private sector organizations to prepare them for current challenges.

A long-time volunteer for ATD, she has served on ASTD's National Board of Directors, was the recipient of the 1992 ASTD Torch Award, the 2004 ASTD Volunteer Staff Partnership Award, the 2006 Gordon Bliss Memorial Award, and in 2012, the inaugural CPLP Fellow Program Honoree from the ASTD Certification Institute. Elaine was instrumental in compiling and revising the CPLP study guides and has designed five ASTD Certificate Programs. She was the 1995 Wisconsin Women Entrepreneur's Mentor Award recipient and has served on the Independent Consultants Association's (ICA) Advisory Committee and the Instructional Systems Association (ISA) Board of Directors. Elaine is currently a member of the Center for Creative Leadership's Board of Governors.

About ATD

The Association for Talent Development (ATD), formerly ASTD, is the world's largest association dedicated to those who develop talent in organizations. These professionals help others achieve their full potential by improving their knowledge, skills, and abilities.

ATD's members come from more than 120 countries and work in public and private organizations in every industry sector.

ATD supports the work of professionals locally in more than 125 chapters, international strategic partners, and global member networks.

1640 King Street
Alexandria, VA 22314
www.td.org
800.628.2783
703.683.8100

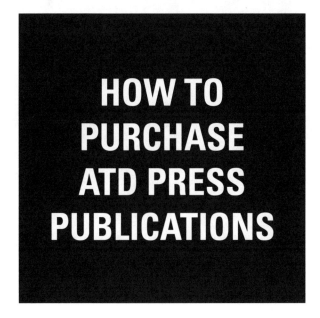

HOW TO PURCHASE ATD PRESS PUBLICATIONS

ATD Press publications are available worldwide in print and electronic format.

To place an order, please visit our online store: www.td.org/books.

Our publications are also available at select online and brick-and-mortar retailers.

Outside the United States, English-language ATD Press titles may be purchased through the following distributors:

United Kingdom, Continental Europe, the Middle East, North Africa, Central Asia, Australia, New Zealand, and Latin America
Eurospan Group
Phone: 44.1767.604.972
Fax: 44.1767.601.640
Email: eurospan@turpin-distribution.com
Website: www.eurospanbookstore.com

Asia
Cengage Learning Asia Pte. Ltd.
Phone: (65)6410-1200
Email: asia.info@cengage.com
Website: www.cengageasia.com

Nigeria
Paradise Bookshops
Phone: 08033075133
Email: paradisebookshops@gmail.com
Website: www.paradisebookshops.com

South Africa
Knowledge Resources
Phone: +27 (11) 706.6009
Fax: +27 (11) 706.1127
Email: sharon@knowres.co.za
Web: www.kr.co.za

For all other territories, customers may place their orders at the ATD online store: **www.td.org/books**.

021514562220

PLANNING A WORKSHOP?
Let us do the heavy lifting...

atd Association for Talent Development

If you loved this book, don't miss additional titles in the ATD Workshop Series!

Each volume includes all the activities, handouts, tools, and assessments you need to create and deliver powerful, effective training.

Preview and order at **td.org/books**.
License content at **td.org/workshopbooks**.

atd Association for Talent Development